THE BIBLE

in Ancient and Modern Media

Biblical Performance Criticism
Orality, Memory, Translation, Rhetoric, Discourse

DAVID RHOADS, EDITOR

The ancient societies of the Bible were overwhelmingly oral. People originally experienced the traditions now in the Bible as oral performances. Focusing on the ancient performance of biblical traditions enables us to shift academic work on the Bible from the mentality of a modern print culture to that of an oral/scribal culture. Conceived broadly, biblical performance criticism embraces many methods as means to reframe the biblical materials in the context of traditional oral cultures, construct scenarios of ancient performances, learn from contemporary performances of these materials, and reinterpret biblical writings accordingly. The result is a foundational paradigm shift that reconfigures traditional disciplines and employs fresh biblical methodologies such as theater studies, speech-act theory, and performance studies. The emerging research of many scholars in this field of study, the development of working groups in scholarly societies, and the appearance of conferences on orality and literacy make it timely to inaugurate this series. For further information on biblical performance criticism, go to www.biblicalperformancecriticism.org.

Books in the Series

Holly Hearon and Philip Ruge-Jones, editors
The Bible in Ancient and Modern Media: Essays in Honor of Tom Boomershine

Forthcoming

David Rhoads
Biblical Performance Criticism: An Emerging Discipline in New Testament Studies

James Maxey
From Orality to Orality: A New Paradigm for Contextual Translation of the Bible

Joanna Dewey
Orality, Scribality, and the Gospel of Mark

Pieter J. J. Botha
Orality and Literacy in Early Christianity

THE BIBLE
in Ancient and Modern Media

Story and Performance

EDITED BY

HOLLY E. HEARON AND
PHILIP RUGE-JONES

CASCADE *Books* · Eugene, Oregon

THE BIBLE IN ANCIENT AND MODERN MEDIA
Story and Performance

Biblical Performance Criticism

Cascade Books
A Division of Wipf and Stock Publishers
199 W. 8th Ave., Suite 3
Eugene, OR 97401

www.wipfandstock.com

ISBN 13: 978-1-55635-990-3

Cataloging-in-Publication data:

The Bible in ancient and modern media : story and performance / edited by Holly E. Hearon and Philip Ruge-Jones.

xxiv + 176 p. ; 23 cm. Includes bibliographic references.

ISBN 13: 978-1-55635-990-3

1. Bible. N.T.—Criticism, interpretation, etc. 2. Bible. N.T.—Performance criticism. 3. Storytelling—Religious aspects—Christianity. 4. Women Storytellers. 5. Storytelling. I. Hearon, Holly E. II. Ruge-Jones, Philip, 1962-. III. Rhoads, David M. IV. Boomershine, Thomas E. V. Title. VI. Series.

BS2555.5 B55 2009

Manufactured in the U.S.A.

These essays are written in honor of Thomas E. Boomershine:
scholar, innovator, storyteller, teacher, friend,
whose commitment to the Gospel has truly been
embodied in word and deed;

On the occasion of the twenty-fifth anniversary of
The Bible in Ancient and Modern Media Section
of the Society of Biblical Literature, 2008

CONTENTS

Contributors · ix

Preface · xi

Introduction: A Passion for Communicating the Gospel · xv
ADAM GILBERT BARTHOLOMEW WITH DAVID RHOADS

PROLOGUE: The Bible in Ancient and Modern Media

1 Why Everything We Know About the Bible Is Wrong: Lessons
from the Media History of the Bible · 3
ROBERT M. FOWLER

PART I: Story and Performance in the Ancient World

2 The Storytelling World of the First Century and the Gospels · 21
HOLLY E. HEARON

3 Women on the Way: A Reconstruction of Late First-Century
Women's Storytelling · 36
JOANNA DEWEY

4 Oral Performance in the New Testament World · 49
WHITNEY SHINER

5 Competing Gospels: Imperial Echoes, A Dissident Voice · 64
ARTHUR J. DEWEY

Contents

PART II: Story and Performance in the Modern World

6   What is Performance Criticism? · 83
DAVID RHOADS

7   The Word Heard: How Hearing a Text Differs from
Reading One · 101
PHILIP RUGE-JONES

8   Life, Story, and the Bible · 114
MARTI J. STEUSSY

9   Taking Place/Taking Up Space · 129
RICHARD W. SWANSON

10   Performing the Living Word: Learnings from a Storytelling
Vocation · 142
DENNIS DEWEY

EPILOGUE: The Bible in Modern Media and Beyond

11   Interpreting the Bible at the Horizon of Virtual New Worlds · 159
A. K. M. ADAM

Selected Bibliography · 175

CONTRIBUTORS

A. K. M. Adam has taught New Testament at Eckerd College, Princeton Theological Seminary, Seabury-Western Theological Seminary, and Duke University. He is the author of several books including *What is Postmodern Biblical Criticism?* and *Faithful Interpretation*, and has edited both *Postmodern Interpretations of the Bible: A Reader*, and *Handbook of Postmodern Biblical Interpretation*. He is an Episcopal priest, and lectures and consults on topics pertaining to technology, theology, and education.

Adam Gilbert Bartholomew is co-founder of the Network of Biblical Storytellers as well as the founding editor and a contributor to the *Journal of Biblical Storytelling*. For twenty years he taught New Testament part-time at Lancaster Theological Seminary. Adam is also now an Episcopal priest.

Arthur J. Dewey is Professor of Theology at Xavier University in Cincinnati, Ohio. A specialist on the historical Jesus and the Gospels, he has written extensively on Paul, the Gospel of Peter, the Gospel of Thomas, the Acts of John, and on the oral, written and electronic gospel. Recent publications include *Spirit and Letter in Paul*. His poetry has appeared in the Christian Century.

Dennis Dewey is a professional "minister of biblical storytelling." An ordained minister of the Presbyterian Church (USA), he has performed and taught at hundreds of venues all over the world. He authored "Great in the Empire of Heaven" in *Preaching the Sermon on the Mount: The World It Imagines*. He has been featured at the National Storytelling Festival, Princeton Theological Seminary's Institute of Theology, the Joseph Campbell Festival, Oxford University, and on national television. Dennis has also served as Executive Director of the Network of Biblical Storytellers and is currently Pastor of Stone Presbyterian Church in Clinton, New York.

Joanna Dewey is the Harvey H. Guthrie, Jr. Professor Emerita of Biblical Studies at Episcopal Divinity School, Cambridge, Massachusetts. A specialist in the Gospel of Mark, orality studies, and feminist approaches to the New Testament, she is the author of several books, including *Mark as Story: An Introduction to the Narrative of a Gospel* (with David Rhoads and Don Michie), and numerous articles, including "From Storytelling to Written Text: The Loss of Early Christian Women's Voices," in *Biblical Theology Bulletin*.

Contributors

Robert M. Fowler is Professor of Religion at Baldwin-Wallace College in Berea, Ohio. He has written extensively on the Gospel of Mark, including his books *Let the Reader Understand: Reader-Response Criticism and the Gospel of Mark,* and *Loaves and Fishes: The Function of Feeding Stories in the Gospel of Mark.*

Holly E. Hearon is Associate Professor of New Testament at Christian Theological Seminary in Indianapolis. She is the author of *The Mary Magdalene Tradition: Witness and Counter-Witness in Early Christian Communities.* She has contributed chapters on storytelling and the relationship between written and spoken word to several books, including *Performing the Gospel: Orality, Memory, and Mark,* and *Jesus, the Voice, and the Text.*

David M. Rhoads is professor of New Testament at the Lutheran School of Theology at Chicago. Rhoads is the author of several books including *Mark as Story: An Introduction to the Narrative of a Gospel* with Joanna Dewey and Don Michie, and *The Challenge of Diversity: The Witness of Paul and the Gospels.* He is completing *Performance Criticism: An Emerging Discipline in New Testament Studies* that will be part of the same series as this current volume. Rhoads is an accomplished performer of biblical writings that include, among others, the Gospel of Mark, Galatians, and Revelation.

Philip Ruge-Jones is Associate Professor of Theology at Texas Lutheran University in Seguin, Texas. He is the author of *The Word of the Cross in a World of Glory, Cross in Tensions: Luther's Theology of the Cross as Theologico-Social Critique,* and has written "Omnipresent, not Omniscient: How Literary Interpretation Confuses the Storyteller's Narrating" in *Between Author and Audience in Mark* (forthcoming).

Whitney T. Shiner is Associate Professor of Religious Studies at George Mason University in Fairfax, Virginia. His research interests include the New Testament and Christian origins, early Christian thought, and world religions. He is the author of *Follow Me! Disciples in Markan Rhetoric,* and *Proclaiming the Gospel: First Century Performance of Mark.*

Marti J. Steussy is the MacAllister-Petticrew Professor of Biblical Interpretation at Christian Theological Seminary in Indianapolis. She began her publishing career with two science fiction novels, but has since focused on the field of biblical studies, most recently by editing and contributing several chapters to *Chalice Introduction to the Old Testament,* and writing *Psalms: Chalice Commentary for Today.*

Richard Swanson is professor of Religion/Philosophy/Classics at Augustana College, Sioux Falls, South Dakota, where he directs the Provoking the Gospel Storytelling Project. He has written *Provoking the Gospel: Methods to Embody Biblical Storytelling Through Drama,* and a series of Pilgrim Press storytelling commentaries including *Provoking the Gospel of Mark, Provoking the Gospel of Luke, Provoking the Gospel of Matthew,* and *Provoking the Gospel of John* (forthcoming).

PREFACE

THE FOLLOWING VOLUME HAS BEEN BROUGHT TOGETHER in honor of Thomas Boomershine, author, scholar, storyteller, and innovator. The particular occasion inviting this recognition of his work is the twenty-fifth anniversary of the Society of Biblical Literature's section on The Bible in Ancient and Modern Media (BAMM), which Tom was instrumental in founding. For two and half decades this program unit has provided scholars with opportunities to explore and experience biblical material in media other than silent print, including both oral and multimedia electronic performances. This book explores many, though by no means all, of the issues lifted up in those sessions over the years.

While some of the authors in this volume speak very personally and specifically about the contribution that Boomershine has made to their own work, all of the authors have benefited from the questions that Tom has continued to raise and the intense conversations they have shared with him. The editors have felt that the best way to honor Tom is by bringing together a volume that will allow new students at undergraduate and early graduate levels to join in the conversation that Tom helped initiate. The chapters in this volume, therefore, invite serious students in the early phase of their religious or theological education to be introduced in an accessible way to the complex issues that BAMM has struggled with over the years. We have insisted that this book be written for the up-and-coming generation of students who will shape thinking about both Bible and media in the years to come. This provided a challenge for us who, as scholars, are accustomed to talking to each other, but we hope you will agree with us that the authors have met this challenge. In the pages of this book, you will discover both the common points of agreement and the areas of contention that are involved in this area of scholarship.

The volume opens with a chapter that will introduce you to the prolific work of Thomas Boomershine. Adam Bartholomew and David

Rhoads offer their insights as Tom's colleagues and close personal friends. In these pages, you will see the tenacity of Boomershine's commitment to reimagining productive ways to understand the Bible's engagement with the world. You will also see the multiple, practical avenues that Tom has pursued in order to facilitate this encounter. You will be inspired by a vocation taken deeply to heart.

In the next chapter, Robert Fowler will guide you through the broad historical sweep of the Bible as it has moved through different dominant forms of media. He divides this process into four phases each of which builds on the forms that proceeded it. He then asks what we need to rethink in terms of our understanding of the Bible in light of this long history.

The next set of chapters explores the ancient media context in which the Bible came to be written. All four authors explore the role and function of orality in the ancient world. Holly Hearon helps us piece together the storytelling context of the ancient world, building on clues from the textual remains of that time period. She shows the centrality of storytelling in the ancient world in both formal and informal contexts with both men and women taking on the storyteller's role. Next Joanna Dewey reconstructs for us a woman's announcement of the good news of Jesus from a generation or two after his ministry took place. Joanna Dewey describes the feminist theory that shapes her work, and then offers an informed and creative narrative designed for performance. Whitney Shiner's chapter then brings our understanding into conversation with rhetorical practices of the ancient world as found in technical manuals of the day. He helps us to understand the performance ideal that was highly prized in the Greco-Roman world. Arthur Dewey shows how Paul's letters can only be understood in the "surround-sound" system of the Roman Empire. As Rome promised a gospel of peace and prosperity through allegiance to the emperor, Paul announced a gospel that challenged imperial claims and honored those whom the empire consistently dishonored.

The next section examines how the knowledge of performance in the ancient world might inform scholarship in our own world. David Rhoads names and describes a new discipline in biblical studies called performance criticism. He leads us through the multiple ways that performing and experiencing others performing open up the impact of the biblical texts for scholars today. Philip Ruge-Jones then shows what was discovered in a college classroom when fifteen students learned the Gospel of

Mark and performed it. He describes how an audience experiences the narrative differently than they would experience a silent reading of the same story. Dennis Dewey shares his own personal vocation as a professional biblical storyteller. He describes the journey that led him to multiple discoveries about the living word through countless performances around the United States and the whole world. Marti Steussy then invites us to reflect on how we shape the stories that we tell and how the stories return the favor by shaping our lives. She invites us to see the complexity of this two-way interaction. Richard Swanson continues the exploration of this complexity by describing what happens when a troupe of players present biblical stories revealing all the cracks and tensions that are contained within it. When the faces of the characters within the biblical drama are seen in their interaction with one another, the biblical stories become stories that invite us into struggles with deep and irresolvable issues that truly matter.

The final section explores how engaging the biblical story in our own multimedia world is provocative. A. K. M. Adam draws us into the digital world and asks what translation of the message of God's word looks like when it moves into this emerging media experience.

May these hints of the movements inspired by Tom Boomershine now be inspiring to you!

HOLLY E. HEARON AND
PHILIP RUGE-JONES

INTRODUCTION

A Passion for Communicating the Gospel:

*An Account of Tom Boomershine as Scholar,
Teacher, and Biblical Storyteller*

Adam Gilbert Bartholomew with David Rhoads

TOM HAD JUST PARKED HIS CAR IN THE GARAGE UNDER VAN
Dusen Hall at Union Theological Seminary in New York City as I was
unloading our moving van. We introduced ourselves and learned that we
were both graduate students in the PhD program in New Testament. It
was September 1968. Tom had completed both his Bachelor of Divinity
and Master of Divinity degrees a few years earlier. He had served a church
in Chicago and was returning to Union to study for a doctorate. Tom, unlike many beginning graduate students, had a very clear project in mind
for his doctoral work: exploring the character of biblical narrative both
as *narrative* rather (than as a mine for theological ideas) and as *originally
oral* in character.

At the time, narrative interpretation of the Bible was just coming
onto the horizon of biblical scholarship. Drawing on the work of secular
literary critics, scholars began to examine the biblical text in relation to
its settings, plot, characters, conflicts, and norms of judgment—exploring
the meaning created in the narrative world itself. Biblical scholarship had
long been dominated by an approach to the Bible called the historical-
critical method. Using this approach, scholars gave careful attention to
the history of the biblical texts as well as to the history behind the texts.
This process required interpreters to break up the narrative into what they

identified as earlier fragments. The writer of the biblical text was viewed as a collector and editor of these earlier fragments or traditions; the biblical scholar was seen as an archaeologist unearthing the layers of accumulated traditions. The narrative criticism that Tom championed claimed these stories in their wholeness, not merely as a museum of various strata of traditions. Tom and others celebrated the integrity of the story world created by the writer of the text, with its own intrinsic value and unique message; through methods of literary interpretation they invited the reader to understand that story world more profoundly.

While narrative critics focused on the story world of the written text, Tom sought to explore these storied texts as stories told in performance. Historical critics had recognized for many years that oral traditions lay behind the biblical text. These were some of the fragments of the tradition that they sought to recover. Yet no one had translated this observation into the actual practice of telling these originally oral stories out loud in order to explore how they might have sounded and how the sound and the experience of hearing the stories told from memory might affect their meaning—nobody until Tom, that is. For all the reasonableness of Tom's idea, it nevertheless seemed strange in the world of biblical scholarship forty years ago.

Tom began to work as a sower scattering seeds in every direction. This strategy has produced a great harvest. He has sown in the academy even when it appeared to be rocky ground; but he has also sown among groups of people in churches, telling them stories from the Bible and teaching them to do the same. Tom has spent his life teaching countless workshops that have enabled individuals and groups to learn how to make storytelling an integral part of the ministry of their church and its mission. Tom has consistently demonstrated the imagination and courage to devote himself to something that people found strange, objectionable, and even embarrassing. Tom has continued to blaze new trails into territory where others still fear greatly to tread, most critically into the realm of the use of electronic media. His concern has always been the communication of the gospel, not just the study of the gospel; indeed the communication of the word of the Bible itself, not just ideas and responses to it. In terms of exploring the latest methods for accomplishing this goal, Tom was and continues to be far ahead of the rest of us. Indeed, if you want to know some things that will hit the scholarly world ten or twenty years from now, pay attention to what is cooking in the mind of Tom Boomershine today!

Unique to Tom's way of telling the stories from the Bible aloud was that he insisted on sticking faithfully to the biblical text itself. Retelling the Bible stories had always been very popular (not among scholars!), but tellers always retold the stories in their own words, or elaborated them, often harmonizing the versions found in different biblical books, or recasting them in the terms of modern culture. Tom's proposal—and discovery—was that the texts themselves were eminently tell-able, an idea often explicitly resisted by people who claimed that the Bible contains mere outlines of stories that would have been greatly expanded when told. Those hearing the power unleashed in Tom's performances of the texts had never heard anything like this before. If these texts lacked life as powerful stories, it was not because they needed more words. What they needed was sound that moved beyond the scholar's dispassionate objectivity and the pious person's sentimentality. This was no easy transformation, since the nonidentical twins of objectivity and sentimentality had for centuries shaped the way Scripture was read in white American and European churches. Tom brought the biblical stories to life by speaking their words, phrases, sentences, and episodes with the sounds suggested or even specified by their content and context. They sounded like the stories we tell each other in daily life, the ones that aim at creating or re-creating an experience rather than giving an objective and merely informative report.

In addition to imagining a whole new way of sounding the narrative texts of the Bible, of reconstituting their dehydrated verbal ciphers as events to be experienced rather than as objective reports to take under advisement, Tom also began to notice their memory-friendly structures. One of his first theses about the biblical versions of the stories was that they are constructed from brief two-, three-, and four-sentence "episodes." Tom spent a great deal of time doing episode analysis by identifying, for example, characteristics of episode beginnings such as changes of time, place, character, and the use of a circumstantial participle. This episodic character of the stories facilitated memory. In addition, groups of episodes often formed small collections that constituted a "section" of the larger narrative. Tom showed how Mark's passion and resurrection narrative is grouped into seven sections, and how within these sections two stories are sometimes brought into relationship with each other. For example, the story of the woman who prophetically anoints Jesus is embedded in the story of the plot to betray Jesus; thus the faithfulness of a stranger is ironically juxtaposed with the unfaithfulness of an intimate friend turned traitor. The story of Peter's denial is interlocked with the story of Jesus' trial before the Sanhedrin, suggesting that the two events occurred simultaneously and that their juxtaposition added Peter's false testimony to that of the other false witnesses. Tom continued to learn, and to tell stories to people, sometimes with a simple guitar accompaniment. Thus he introduced a new paradigm for the role biblical texts play in the communication of meaning, moving from the text as referent to the text as medium for the generating of experience.

Tom's dissertation was on Mark's passion and resurrection narrative. Drawing on Wayne Booth's categories of literary analysis, he analyzed the biblical text in terms of plot, characterization, narrative comments, and verbal threads. These are familiar categories today, but they were new to biblical scholars at the time. He also memorized the Greek text and did something not just new, but radical in biblical scholarship. He first made a tape recording of a reading that imitated the typical way a lesson would be read in a church on Sunday; then he recorded a telling of the same story from memory in a style typical of storytelling. The difference was striking. The passion narrative had a new sound and feel to it! The drama of the story engaged listeners and had a direct impact on them. When Tom performed "The Passion Story," the hearer felt passion! By combining the art of storytelling with the cutting edge media of the 1970s, the cassette tape recorder, Tom began his plunge into the use of electronic media to communicate the gospel. This breakthrough foreshadowed his later achievements of establishing a Doctor of Ministry degree in electronic media at United Theological Seminary and of founding first Lumicon, a corporation dedicated to producing resources for Bible study and communication in electronic media, and then the GoTell Web site with electronic resources online for scriptural study.

The beginning of the next episode in Tom's story was marked by a terrible accident. Tom had recently become professor of New Testament at New York Theological Seminary. Shortly thereafter, he was walking around the back of his car to pay for the gas he had just pumped when another car pulled in behind his and, instead of stopping, slid into him on some oil on the blacktop. He was pinned between the bumpers of his car and the other car, which nearly cut off both his legs. For the next months he lay in terrible pain and humiliation in the hospital. A major resource for his endurance was retelling himself Mark's story of Jesus' death and resurrection. Tom's suspicion regarding the power of these stories for personal transformation was confirmed as the story of Jesus' death and resurrection became the vessel that held his own sense of loss, as well as the source of his own healing.

The Network of Biblical Storytellers was conceived around this time as Tom began to share his dream of a "network of Biblical storytellers." He imagined people throughout the world who would learn by heart and tell the stories of the people of God in many different settings—worship, teaching, pastoral care, evangelism, administration, and social justice—in order to bring to the world the gospel of Jesus Christ. In other words, he envisioned the church as a community in which the stories would be learned and shared by every person in every dimension of the community's life and mission. This dream has guided him and many of us privileged to share it with him on a wonderful story journey. From the first chapter meeting of biblical storytellers at New York Theological Seminary to later intense weekend seminars, a community was formed that began experimenting with new methods for learning a story appropriate to different learning styles (visual, oral-aural, kinesthetic), trying out diverse ways of retelling the stories in poetry, mime, dialogue, and eventually video.

In 1985, a national biblical storytelling festival was held at Biddeford Pool, Maine, that became first a biennial and then annual event. At that festival we decided to incorporate, and a board of directors for the network was formed. When Tom moved to United Seminary in Dayton, Ohio, the Network began to grow and serve as a crucible for the continuing work of Christians of multiple denominations from the ranks of clergy, laity, and scholars who believed in the power of these stories. One of the great milestones of Tom's work growing out of the Network, by now dubbed "NOBS," was the publication by Abingdon Press of his book *Story Journey*. This book laid out the methodology Tom had developed for all who were interested in learning to tell biblical stories. He made the revolutionary move at that time of offering a cassette recording of the book. Abingdon was skeptical that the book would sell. Decades later, it is still in print and may be the book holding the record for the longest run of any of Abingdon's publications. In all this work, Tom has shown his commitment to make scholarship accessible to the people. But he was also discovering ways in which the people can contribute to scholarly endeavors. Every year people from all over the United States and the world gather for several days to tell each other biblical stories, to support each others' ministries, to challenge each other on the shape of faithfulness, and to worship God with the primary language of our faith: stories.

The success with NOBS did not cause Tom to give up on his dream of affecting biblical scholarship as a discipline. He held on to the vision that the oral performance of the biblical narrative meant that everything must be rethought in biblical scholarship. In particular, he sought to make an impact on the main organization of biblical scholars from the academy, The Society of Biblical Literature (SBL). Tom played a key role in establishing the SBL group The Bible in Ancient and Modern Media (BAMM). Tom's work on the performance of the passion narrative meant that he understood the paradigmatic shift in media from oral culture to literary culture that was beginning to take place in ancient times. He saw that in our own day we were undergoing an equally important shift from print culture to the new electronic media. This SBL seminar created a gathering that took seriously the many directions of Tom's scholarly work. In 2008, BAMM celebrates its twenty-fifth anniversary. The number of other seminars and sessions that have since formed within SBL that might be considered offshoots of BAMM is testament to the visionary nature of BAMM's beginning. Once again Tom anticipated important shifts in the scholarly world by ten and twenty years. In recent years, Tom has created the NOBS Seminar. This group meets annually bringing together biblical scholars largely from BAMM and skilled storytellers from NOBS to see what they can discover together that they would not otherwise see alone.

Tom's accomplishments are too many to expound in this short chapter, but several still deserve mention. NOBS, together with Tom, has moved in global directions with early travel to the Soviet Union and, more recently, with organizing events in England, Australia, and Gambia. In the early nineties, Tom convinced the American Bible Society to gather a team of scholars and to produce videos and interactive computer resources of three New Testament stories: *Out of the Tombs, Mary's Song,* and *A Father and Two Sons.* The origin of this project was Tom's dissatisfaction with previous videos of biblical stories, in which the images are in command and the text is adjusted to the capacities of the images. One day it occurred to Tom that MTV videos place the text of a song in command and that images are drawn into the video by association with the text.

MTV thus provided the genre for these Bible story videos! This genre expresses the shift from linear to associative thinking.

At United Theological Seminary, Tom also established a Doctor of Ministry Program in Biblical Storytelling that has brought into the enterprise of storytelling some very remarkable people, many of whom have brought their gifts into NOBS. Tom has taught generations of men and women to live faithfully and well. More than all else, what must be said is that underlying all of Tom's work is a passionate commitment to justice and peace in the world. This lies behind his focus on sharing stories of peace and love and mercy and justice, of goodness and forgiveness and reconciliation. It was the basis for the mission of NOBS. This same passion is behind his scholarly efforts to combat anti-Semitism. It fuels his commitment to reach so many people living in an electronic culture with the good news of the gospel.

One of the greatest blessings of Tom's life has been his partnership with his wife, Amelia. She served for a time as coordinator of the Network of Biblical Storytellers, converted *NOBS NEWS* into *The Biblical Storyteller*, and then she worked together with Tom in establishing both Lumicon and GoTell, as means to produce electronic-media resources for the communication of the Bible. She has shared his vision when others were not ready to join him; she has helped him take the practical steps necessary to make his dreams a reality.

Tom's work over the years has been truly astonishing. He is always seeing connections between the most disparate things and people. The move from the re-appropriation of the biblical texts as stories, which were read and told aloud in a lively and experience-generating manner, led naturally, but not necessarily, to the exploration of electronic means for communicating the stories. Tom brings together pastors, Christian educators, storytellers, biblical scholars, oral-tradition scholars, translators, video producers, and publishers, both in the United States and internationally. He integrates prayer and storytelling and scholarship and the arts and contemporary issues. The scope of his imagination and his courage to try to bring into actuality what he is imagining is amazing and never stops expanding. We have benefited professionally, spiritually, and personally from the profound friendship and partnership we have shared with this caring, visionary man.

Tom stands out as one who has brought the church and the academy into the new world being born out of the revolution in communications through electronic media. His vision is prophetic. He has conceived a new generation of Christian evangelists, planted seeds, nurtured the tender shoots that have sprung from them, and often suffered the disappointment of seeing the crop fail. The origin of it all is his passionate love of God as he has come to know God through the narratives of the Bible and his passionate love for God's world and all of God's children—a love that God has implanted and nurtured in him. As we move into the future, our prayer is this: Out of the seeds Tom has been planting and out of the young plants he has been tending and even out of the losses he and Amelia have endured, may God bring an astonishing harvest for the sake of God's whole creation.

Published Writings and Recordings
of Thomas E. Boomershine[1]

"The Writing on the Wall: Telling the Story in a Digital World." 2005 NOBS Festival Gathering Keynotes. *The Journal of Biblical Storytelling* 15 (2006) 5–33. (Published by the Network of Biblical Storytellers International, 1000 West 42nd Street, Indianapolis, IN 46208–3301.)

"Mel, Go to Seminary, Please: A Biblical Storyteller's Reflection on 'the Passion of the Christ.'" *Journal of Theology (United Theological Seminary)* 109 (2005) 17–30.

"Biblical Storytelling and Biblical Scholarship." *The Journal of Biblical Storytelling* 12 (2002–2003) 5–13

"Toward a Biblical Theology of Communication." *Catholic International Quarterly* (Fall 2001).

"Does United Methodism Have a Future in an Electronic Culture?" In *United Methodism and American Culture Volume 4: Questions for the Twenty-First Century Church*, edited by Russell E. Richey and Dennis Campbell, 79–90, 328–29. Nashville: Abingdon, 1999.

"The Polish Cavalry and Christianity in Electronic Culture." *Journal of Theology (United Theological Seminary)* 99 (1995) 90–102.

"Jesus of Nazareth and the Watershed of Ancient Orality and Literacy." *Semeia* 65 (1994) 7–36.

"A Transmediatization Theory of Biblical Translation." *United Bible Societies Bulletin* 170/171 (1994) 49–57.

"Biblical Megatrends: Towards a Paradigm for the Interpretation of the Bible in Electronic Media." In *American Bible Society Symposium Papers on the Bible in the Twenty-First Century*, edited by Howard Clark Kee, 209–30. Philadelphia: Trinity, 1993.

"Biblical Storytelling in Education." *Journal of Christian Education* 36 (1993) 7–18.

"Out of the Tombs: A Scripture Translation of Mark 5:1–20." Videorecording. 9 min. USA: American Bible Society, 1991.

---

1. Assembled by Cortney L. Haley.

Introduction

"Doing Theology in the Electronic Age: The Meeting of Orality and Electricity." *Journal of Theology (United Theological Seminary)* 95 (1991) 4–14.

"Biblical Translation and Communication Technology." *United Bible Societies Bulletin* 160/161 (1991) 14–19.

"New Paradigm for Interpreting the Bible on Television." In *Changing Channels: The Church and the Television Revolution*, edited by Tyron Inbody, 61–76. Dayton, OH: Whaleprints, 1990.

"Telling the Gospel." *Journal of Biblical Storytelling* 2 (1990) 27–34.

"Christian Community and Technologies of the Word." In *Communicating Faith in a Technological Age*, edited by James McDonnell and Frances Trampiets, 84–103. Middlegreen, Slough, England: St. Paul Publishing, 1989.

"The Reemergence of Biblical Narrative." *Journal of Biblical Storytelling* 1 (1989) 6–15.

"Biblical Storytelling in the City." In *Urban Church Education*, edited by Donald B. Rogers, 142–51. Birmingham, AL: Religious Education Press, 1989.

"Epistemology at the Turn of the Ages in Paul, Jesus, and Mark: Rhetoric and Dialectic in Apocalyptic and the New Testament." In *Apocalyptic and the New Testament: Essays in Honor of J. Louis Martyn*, edited by Joel Marcus and Marion L. Soards, 147–67. Journal for the Study of the New Testament Supplements 24. Sheffield: JSOT Press, 1989.

Story Journey Sound Recording: An Invitation to the Gospels as Storytelling. Nashville: Abingdon, 1988.

Story Journey: An Invitation to the Gospels as Storytelling. Nashville: Abingdon, 1988.

"The Birth of Jesus: Telling the Story That Connects with Us Here and Now." *Circuit Rider* (1988) 12–14.

"Peter's Denial as Polemic or Confession: The Implications of Media Criticism." *Semeia* 39 (1987) 47–68.

"Religious Education and Media Change: A Historical Sketch." *Religious Education* 82 (1987) 269–78.

"John the Baptist." Videorecording. 30 min. USA: United Theological Seminary, 1984.

"Christianity in Ancient and Modern Media." Videorecording. USA: United Theological Seminary, 1982.

"Mark 16:8 and the Apostolic Commission." *Journal of Biblical Literature* 100 (1981) 225–39.

"The Narrative Technique of Mark 16:8." *Journal of Biblical Literature* 100 (1981) 213–23. Joint authorship with (Adam) Gilbert L. Bartholomew.

"An Introduction to the Synoptic Gospels: Four Gospel Stories." Videorecording. 50 min. USA: United Theological Seminary, 1980.

"Introduction to the New Testament Greek Alphabet." Videorecording. 30 min. USA: United Theological Seminary, 1980.

"Introduction to Greek Tools for Exegesis." Videorecording. 30 min. USA: United Theological Seminary, 1980.

"An Introduction to Exegesis Videorecording." Videorecording. 30 min. USA: United Theological Seminary, 1980.

"The Structure of Narrative Rhetoric in Genesis 2–3." *Semeia* 18 (1980) 113–29.

"Das Erzählen biblischer Geschichten." *Wege zum Menschen* 28 (1976) 470–73. Joint authorship with (Adam) Gilbert L. Bartholomew.

"Theological Education: Rich Man's Slave or Poor Man's Servant?" *Katallagete* 2 (1969) 34–40.

Prologue

The Bible in Ancient and Modern Media

1

WHY EVERYTHING WE KNOW ABOUT THE BIBLE IS WRONG

Lessons from the Media History of the Bible

ROBERT M. FOWLER

THE FIRST BIBLE I EVER OWNED WAS GIVEN TO ME FIFTY years ago by my grandparents, back home in Kansas, on Easter Sunday 1958. Although I have not used it seriously in decades, it still sits on a shelf in my study. When I take it down now and open it, I see my grandmother's handwriting, filling the blank lines on the "Presented To" page conveniently provided by the publisher inside the front cover: "Presented To: Bobby Fowler, By: Grandma and Grandpa Fowler, Date: Easter, April 6, 1958." This Bible is a King James Bible (first published in 1611), a red-letter edition (all the words of Jesus, from Matthew through Revelation, printed in red ink), and small in size (approximately 4 ½" x 6 ½"). It is handsomely bound in black leather, and it once had a zipper with which to enclose the pages for protection. The zipper is now broken, and the black leather has lost much of its suppleness, but its once strong, intoxicating aroma still lingers faintly. My name (a more formal "Robert Fowler") is imprinted in gold on the front cover. The Old Testament takes up 800 pages of fine print, and the New Testament, 246 pages.

I would hardly have known at the age of seven that this Bible is definitely a Protestant Bible: containing 66 books, it lacks the books of the Apocrypha that would be found in a Roman Catholic or Eastern Orthodox Bible. For years I carried this Bible to Sunday School and church, and this was the Bible I read in my first fumbling efforts at Bible reading. However,

I never fell in love with the strange, archaic wording of the King James Version, and as soon as I was introduced to modern translations (such as the Revised Standard Version), I was happy to make the leap to Bibles that were more easily understood. Indeed, my most vivid memory of the contents of my first Bible is of its colorful illustrations, not its words. My Bible was published by the World Publishing Company, Cleveland, Ohio, which made no impression upon me years ago in Kansas, but which strikes me as ironic today, since I have spent most of my career teaching at a liberal arts college in a Cleveland suburb. Apparently, a Bible printed in Cleveland started me on a path that eventually led me, from the farm in Kansas, to teaching college Bible courses minutes away from where my first Bible was printed.

What did the experience of handling (e.g., carrying to church, zipping and unzipping, smelling the rich aroma of the leather, etc.), to say nothing of the experience of opening and reading this Bible (or just looking at its pictures and my grandmother's inscription), teach me about the Bible? What impressions were left upon me, and upon countless other readers of the Bible, by repeated encounters with printed Bibles such as my beloved KJV? Here are some of the lessons, both explicit and implicit, that I learned:

1. The Bible is a *written*, indeed, a *printed book*.

2. The Bible is a *single* book, completely enclosed between two covers.

3. The Bible was written *for me*. (My family and my Sunday School teachers urged me to read my Bible and to apply it to my life—suggesting it was intended for me. It is written in my language, English, although the English of the King James Bible is strange and hard to understand. And my Bible has my name imprinted on the front cover—it was obviously intended for me!)

4. *The contents of the Bible are fixed, unchanging, frozen in amber, forever.*

5. The *Bible is "the Word of God."* (I never found this claim made explicitly anywhere in the Bible, but it was an impression I received from the claims made about the Bible in Sunday school classrooms and in worship services. Also, all those words of Jesus in red ink really impressed me.)

I will suggest in this essay that for the last five hundred years, ever since Johann Gutenberg's invention of the printing press in the 1450s, lessons such as these have been shaped largely by the fact that we were reading, not just the Bible, but *a printed* Bible. Holding in our hands and doing the countless things we do with a printed Bible engrains lessons within us of which we are typically not aware. However, the history of the Bible goes back 2500 years before Gutenberg, to at least 1000 BCE. The oldest contents of both the Hebrew Bible and New Testament were communicated orally, exclusively, without benefit of writing. Then, even when biblical books began to be written on parchment or papyrus, few people could afford to own them, few people could read them, and most people would have still experienced biblical material as live oral/aural (=speaking/hearing) performance. It was only when the printing press was invented that people could begin to imagine owning their own Bible and being able to learn to read it and heed it for themselves. This is what I am getting at in my brash title, "Why Everything We Know About the Bible is Wrong." Because we have been reading the Bible in print for 500 years, we naturally assume that that is the way people have always experienced the Bible. But that is not the case: for 2500 years prior to Gutenberg, most people experienced the Bible either through oral/aural performance or in the form of unique and rare handwritten manuscripts. If we want to understand how the contents of the Bible were first experienced and understood by ancient Jews and Christians, then we need to gain an understanding of the media history of the Bible prior to Gutenberg.[1]

For the sake of convenience, the history of communication media can be divided into four eras:[2]

1. Oral/Aural Communication

2. Manuscript Communication

3. Print Communication

4. Electronic Communication

1. Tom Boomershine has been a pioneer in the exploration of the media history of the Bible; see his "Biblical Megatrends: Towards a Paradigm for the Interpretation of the Bible in Electronic Media," in *American Bible Society Symposium Papers on the Bible in the Twenty-First Century*, ed. Howard Clark Kee (Philadelphia: Trinity, 1993) 209–30.

2. Walter J. Ong, *Orality and Literacy: The Technologizing of the Word* (London: Methuen, 1982).

Oral/Aural Communication

It is impossible to tell how long humans have had the physical capability and the cultural inclination to engage in oral communication. Estimates made by paleoanthropologists vary from 50,000 years to several million years.[3] Since writing was only invented a few thousand years ago, this means that for most of human history on planet Earth, humans have communicated by the spoken word only. Even after writing was invented, oral/aural communication continued to be the primary means of communication for most people. For thousands of years, literacy was limited to an elite, privileged few, and even today the most literate and bookish of persons will typically use spoken language throughout the course of a day. Writing has never completely replaced speaking and never will. However, once writing was invented, it began a slow, steady march toward eventual dominance over speech, if not in practice, then at least in theory. Fair or not, many persons in modernity have harbored a prejudice in favor of written language over spoken language. Like many of our other current attitudes toward communication media, such prejudice probably arises from our five centuries of experience with the printed book.

Anthropologists and other researchers learned a great deal about oral/aural cultures in the twentieth century, often from investigating cultures where oral/aural communication had remained the dominant means of communication, in spite of thousands of years of writing. For example, Milman Parry and Albert Lord studied oral storytelling in Yugoslavia in the 1930s, uncovering striking similarities between those 20th century oral performances and what we can infer about oral performances in the ancient world, such as Homer's performances of the epic poems known as the *Iliad* and the *Odyssey*.[4] While we do not have space here to discuss the various characteristics of oral/aural culture,[5] we must note one especially important characteristic. In spite of the cultural conservatism of many oral/aural cultures, their practice of oral communication is at the same time open, flexible, and fluid. To put it sharply, in an oral culture

---

3. Donald Johanson, Blake Edgar, and David L. Brill, *From Lucy to Language*, rev. ed. (New York: Simon & Schuster, 2006) 106–7.

4. Albert B. Lord, *The Singer of Tales*, Harvard Studies in Comparative Literature 24 (Cambridge: Harvard University Press, 1960).

5. For a convenient summary of the major characteristics of oral/aural culture, see Ong, *Orality and Literacy*, 31–77.

typically no two performances of a story are ever identical. It is taken for granted that the oral storyteller will vary his or her language in response to the needs of the moment, responding to the particular time, place, and audience. Exact, precise repetition of words is what a person from print culture might hope for or expect, but that is because the printing press (or its electronic descendents, such as the photocopying machine) allows us to reproduce printed marks on paper endlessly, with exactitude and precision. People in an oral/aural culture, by contrast, expect and invariably receive from the oral storyteller a slightly (or greatly!) different story every time a story is told. Whereas a deeply literate person might compose a story, memorize it, and perform it as faithfully as possible to the original text, in an oral/aural culture there is no such thing as an "original" composition that is memorized and then repeated verbatim. Rather, each performance of a story is itself a unique, new composition.

The Oral/Aural Bible

What might it mean to speak of "the Bible" in the historical era of exclusive oral/aural communication? We do not know how much of the Bible originated as spoken word only—probably much more than we imagine. It has long been suspected that such foundational material as the legends of Genesis and the parables of Jesus originated as oral storytelling. Only with the passage of time—centuries, in the case of Genesis, and decades, in the case of the parables of Jesus—did these narratives find their way into written form. It is rather amazing to modern, printed-book–literate folk to contemplate that, as far we know, Jesus never wrote a word of his teaching, nor did he ever command anyone else to do so. Ancient oral/aural peoples were comfortable enough with the spoken word to get by with it for vast ages of human history. Even after the Israelite scribes had been writing for a millennium, a teacher such as Jesus was perfectly comfortable operating in a purely oral/aural mode.

It is a controversial claim, and impossible to demonstrate conclusively, but maybe Jesus *did not* write down his teachings because he *could not*—perhaps he could neither read nor write.[6] Does that suggestion

6. The only place in the gospels where Jesus is portrayed reading is in the synagogue scene in Luke 4:16-30. It is quite possible that the unquestionably literate author, Luke, imagined here a hypothetically literate protagonist, Jesus. Sometimes it is claimed that Jesus was writing something on the ground in John 8:6, 8, as he waited for a decision

offend us? Do we bristle at the thought of an "illiterate" Jesus?[7] If so, why? After all, the passages in the gospels that might be cited to make the case that Jesus was literate are few and far between. Granted, an illiterate Jesus would probably offend many believers on purely theological grounds ("how could the Messiah, the Son of God, not be able to read or write?"), but isn't the real problem here the modern prejudice in favor of literacy? The printed word is so widespread and deeply engrained in our culture that it is exceedingly hard for us to imagine that vast portions of the Bible were once exclusively oral, not written at all, and thus, once upon a time, "the Bible" was not a book. It is also hard for us to imagine that a central figure of the Bible might not have possessed the capability to read and write, a capability that we take for granted in our own time.

If it is hard for us to imagine biblical traditions originating as purely oral communication, it is all the more difficult to comprehend that this language would have shared the characteristics of oral performance that we have discovered in the past century. For example, because oral performance is never exactly the same thing twice, when the legends of Genesis or the parables of Jesus were performed, they were different every time. The idea that oral communication was fluid and changeable bewilders and frightens many printed-book–literate people. ("If it changes every time, how can we trust it?") Even when we discover multiple versions of certain stories written in Genesis, or when we find different variations of the parables of Jesus preserved in the gospels, we may still insist that there surely must have been a single "original" version of these stories. However, that is an attitude that comes from print culture, not from oral culture. Were we literate folk to live in an oral culture, our bewilderment and apprehension would surely decrease, and we would probably learn how to trust communication that is inherently fluid and changeable.

---

about who would cast the first stone at the woman charged with adultery. However, the Greek here is ambiguous; *katagraphō* or *graphō* may simply mean "scratch, etch, or engrave." In other words, he may simply have been doodling in the dust, and not necessarily "writing" anything. For a plausible argument that a first-century Galilean peasant such as Jesus was most likely illiterate, see John Dominic Crossan, *Jesus: A Revolutionary Biography* (San Francisco: HarperSanFrancisco, 1994) 25–26.

7. Let us be clear that "illiterate" is a biased term, since it presumes that literacy is the norm, and that to be without literacy is to be somehow lacking or deficient. If a person (or an entire culture) practices oral communication exclusively, it is unfair to judge them on the basis of the absence of literacy.

Manuscript Communication

We turn now to the invention of writing. Different writing systems were invented at different times and places in the ancient world, but in Western culture we tend to look back to the writing systems invented in ancient Mesopotamia and Egypt, apparently in the fourth millennium BCE.[8] Best known of these writing systems are cuneiform in Mesopotamia, and hieroglyphics in Egypt. In the second millennium BCE, the Western alphabet was invented somewhere in the Middle East. It is generally believed that the Phoenicians spread the use of this Semitic alphabet throughout the Mediterranean. The alphabet originally consisted of consonants only, and even today Semitic languages such as Hebrew and Arabic are regularly written without vowel markings. When the Greeks obtained the alphabet in the eighth century BCE, they added the vowels to the consonants, thus creating the version of the alphabet that is the precursor of all modern Western alphabets.

The word *manuscript* simply means, "written by hand." It has nothing to do with the material on which the writing is done. In antiquity such writing materials included stone, wood, clay, papyrus, and parchment. For thousands of years, all writing was manuscript or handwriting. Only when the printing press came along did people begin to produce "typographic" writing, or writing by means of a machine.

Given the modern aspiration to achieve universal literacy, it is hard to imagine that for thousands of years the ability to read and write was limited to an elite, privileged few. William V. Harris estimates that in the Greco-Roman period, no more than 10 to 20 percent of the population could read or write.[9] This means that for thousands of years after the invention of writing, most people continued to live in a primarily oral/aural world, until Gutenberg's invention arrived and began to encourage literacy to a degree never before imaginable. It is little wonder, then, that many of the practices and attitudes of oral/aural culture continued in manuscript culture. For example, manuscripts were often not written by the hand of the author, but rather dictated by the author to a secretary.[10] If read, a

8. For this and other points here, see "Writing," in Paul J. Achtemeier, gen. ed., *HarperCollins Bible Dictionary* (San Francisco: HarperSanFrancisco, 1996) 1227–30.

9. William V. Harris, *Ancient Literacy* (Cambridge: Harvard University Press, 1989).

10. It is well known that the apostle Paul regularly dictated his letters to a secretary. One of his secretaries, Tertius, appends his own greetings at end of the letter to the Romans (Rom 16:22).

manuscript was typically read aloud, not silently. Manuscripts, however, were often not read, but rather memorized, and then "consulted" mentally or recited from memory. This means that many of the quotations of Jewish Scripture that we find in the New Testament may be citations from memory, not from having a written copy of a biblical book open on a desk, in front of the author.

Just as many practices of orality were preserved in manuscript culture, so too were the attitudes of orality maintained. This includes the understanding of language that we discussed above, namely, that language is fluid and changeable. Just as no two oral performances were ever the same, no two manuscript copies of a book were ever alike. Since all of the materials used in making a manuscript were produced by hand, there was no consistency or uniformity in writing surfaces, no standard page sizes, no standard tints of ink. Also, the scribes who wrote the manuscripts exercised tremendous freedom both in writing the original manuscript and in "correcting" (adding to or subtracting from) that same manuscript years later. As noted before, our experience of the printed page leads us to expect that each copy of a biblical book could and should be identical to every other copy, but this kind of exact reproduction of writing was impossible to achieve before the invention of the printing press.

The Manuscript Bible

The oldest surviving manuscripts of biblical books are written, of course, not in English, and especially not in King James English, but in ancient forms of Hebrew, Aramaic (only a few passages in the Hebrew Bible), and Greek. Although Jews have sometimes translated their Scriptures, translation has been an especially Christian enterprise from the very beginnings of Christianity up to the present. Even so, Christians have repeatedly forgotten that their Bibles are usually not written in the original biblical languages but instead are translations from the ancient languages into contemporary, vernacular languages. Huge misunderstandings arise when people naively assume that their Bible is a faithful copy of the one and only original Bible, however that might be understood. If our Bible is not written in the languages used by the biblical authors, it is clear that we are not reading a faithful copy of the original.

There are additional ways in which the dream of the one and only true original is undermined. For one thing, no autograph copy (*the* original copy of a manuscript, penned by the author or his secretary) exists for any biblical book.[11] Thus, even if we could read the Bible in the ancient versions of Hebrew, Aramaic, and Greek in which it was written, we still could not read the original copies, because they no longer exist. The surviving manuscripts that we do have are copies of copies of copies—and no two of these are ever the same. Why? For one thing, because no two handmade items are ever identical. Also, the scribes who did the copying felt free to add or subtract from the wording they had received. And because, as fallible humans, these scribes sometimes made mistakes in copying. Again, the precision and accuracy in reproduction that came with the printing press was impossible and unthinkable in the era of the manuscript.

There are still other ways in which the experience of the Bible in manuscript form strikes us today as quite peculiar. Among early New Testament manuscripts, it is the norm for manuscripts to contain only a single book or at most a portion of the New Testament—for example, the letters of Paul or perhaps all four gospels. However, it is extremely rare to find a complete New Testament in manuscript form.[12] Ancient biblical manuscripts, such as Codex Vaticanus or Sinaiticus, which contain not only the whole New Testament but also the Old Testament (in the Septuagint Greek translation), are extremely rare. Why? Because such large manuscripts are simply too labor-intensive and expensive to produce, to say nothing of them being cumbersome to use, because of their immense size. It is only with the appearance of the printing press that it becomes feasible to have all the books of the Bible conveniently enclosed between two covers, and in a user-friendly size.

Print Communication

From here on I am going to be briefer, because as we move into the cultures of print and electronic communication, we move into much more familiar territory. And yet, at the same time, precisely because these

11. Harry Y. Gamble, *Books and Readers in the Early Church: A History of Early Christian Texts* (New Haven: Yale University Press, 1995) 42.

12. Ibid., 67–69.

modes of communication are so familiar to us, they are mostly invisible to us: we tend to see through them, rather than to see them for what they are. As I have argued throughout this essay, when we think of the Bible, we tend to think of the printed Bible, but we are often oblivious to the lessons that the use of the printed Bible teaches us. This is hardly surprising, given that we are not especially aware of the countless ways in which the printing press has shaped our whole culture. Elizabeth L. Eisenstein has documented the immense impact of print in shaping the modern world, the world we have lived in for the last few centuries.[13] Among the many results of the widespread use of the printed book, Eisenstein identifies the following:

- With the mass production of cheaper books, widespread literacy at last became both imaginable and achievable

- Printing provided the technology necessary to better preserve old knowledge, to correct mistaken knowledge, and to expand new knowledge

- Thus the printing press served to spark the development of modern scientific and historical investigation

- It also promoted cultural and religious ferment, such as with the Renaissance and the Protestant Reformation

- It encouraged the use of vernacular European languages, and it led to the standardization of these languages

- With the promotion of vernacular languages, nationalistic identities were encouraged

In many ways, these and other observations made by Eisenstein describe the world in which we still live today, and thus we are still inhabitants of the "Gutenberg Galaxy."[14] More precisely, we live in "The Late Age of Print,"[15] at the same time that we are making a transition into the new Electronic Age.

---

13. Elizabeth L. Eisenstein, *The Printing Press as an Agent of Change: Communications and Cultural Transformations in Early Modern Europe*, 2 vols. (Cambridge: Cambridge University Press, 1979).

14. Marshall McLuhan, *The Gutenberg Galaxy: The Making of Typographic Man* (Toronto: University of Toronto Press, 1962).

15. Jay David Bolter, *Writing Space: The Computer, Hypertext, and the History of Writing* (Hillsdale, NJ: Erlbaum, 1991) 2.

The Printed Bible

With the invention of the printing press, it became possible to print texts of the Hebrew and Greek testaments, which facilitated a rebirth of knowledge of these ancient languages among Christian scholars. That in turn led to an explosion of vernacular biblical translations within a century of Gutenberg. In producing those printed vernacular Bibles, it became a simple matter to put all the books of the Bible together between two covers, a practice almost unheard of in manuscript culture. It also became possible to produce copies of the Bible in massive quantities and to distribute them inexpensively, far and wide. This lured people into thinking that they really ought to learn to read, so they could read these new Bibles for themselves. This impulse toward literacy and individual Bible reading went hand in hand with the historical emergence of the Bible-oriented version of Christianity known as Protestantism. For the first time in the history of the Bible, it was feasible to read and heed the Bible for oneself, a peculiarly modern and individualistic form of the Christian faith.

Electronic Communication

To state the obvious, this is where most of us live today, in networks of digital, electronic communication. Whether we are surfing the Web, pushing the buttons on an ATM machine, watching television, or talking on our cell phones, we are immersed in electronic media the way that fish swim in the sea. Of the many things that could be said here about electronic communication, we will focus on just one important aspect.

When new communication media come along, the old media do not vanish. For example, when writing was invented, people did not stop talking, and when printing was invented, we did not stop writing with pen on paper. Instead of the old media fading away, the introduction of a radically new communication medium requires that the whole array of available communication tools, old and new alike, undergo a radical reorganization. Such a reorganization of communication possibilities is taking place today with the electronic media. Unlike previous media revolutions, the electronic media not only allow a place for all the older forms of media, they actually reenact all of those older media. Think of the oral/aural communication that we engage in when we talk on our cell phones. Think of the handwriting we can do when we "paint" or "draw" on the computer screen using a computer mouse or an electronic tablet and stylus. Think of the imitation of the printing press made possible by our word-processing software and a laser printer. Without question, the electronic communication media have made possible new, unprecedented, and extraordinary communication experiences (for example, surfing the Web from anywhere in the world or finding our physical location on the planet via the Global Positioning System). But the electronic media also allow the old media to live again in ways we could never have anticipated.

Walter Ong, the great scholar of media history, observed that with electronic media we are moving into an age of "secondary orality," an experience of electronically facilitated oral/aural communication reminiscent of "primary orality," the ancient oral/aural culture before writing was invented.[16] Writing and print still loom large in our world, but we are just as likely to chat with our friends on the phone or by means of a video link on our computers. In school we are still taught to write by hand, and we learn how to word process and print handsome pages of text, but when we want to ask Dad for financial assistance, we are more likely to pick up the phone than to write a letter. Rather than get our news from reading a newspaper, we might choose instead to watch TV or listen to the radio. Obviously, we will never return to the days of primary orality, as if writing had never existed, but many aspects of ancient orality have re-emerged in a communications environment of electronically aided orality.

The Electronic Bible

At the dawn of the Electronic Age, it is impossible to say into what forms the Bible will mutate.[17] Already, however, there have been significant experiments, exploring the possibilities of electronic media for the Bible. I will mention only one, the New Media Bible Project of the American

16. Ong, *Orality and Literacy*; Robert M. Fowler, "How the Secondary Orality of the Electronic Age Can Awaken Us to the Primary Orality of Antiquity, or, What Hypertext Can Teach Us About the Bible," *Interpersonal Computing and Technology: An Electronic Journal for the 21st Century* 2.3 (1994) 12–46. Available online at http://www.helsinki.fi/science/optek/1994/n3/fowler.txt.

17. For some speculation, see Fowler, "The End of the Bible As We Know It: The Metamorphosis of the Biblical Traditions in the Electronic Age," in *Literary Encounters with the Reign of God: Festschrift for Robert C. Tannehill*, ed. Paul Kim and Sharon Ringe (New York: T. & T. Clark, 2004) 341–56.

Bible Society.[18] During the decade of the 1990s, ABS carried out an extensive experiment in "translating" Bible stories into electronic media. By the end of the project, six videos had been produced: *Out of the Tombs* (Mark 5:1-20), *The Visit* (Luke 1:39-56), *A Father and Two Sons* (Luke 15:11-32), *The Neighbor* (Luke 10:25-37), *Resurrection* (John 20:1-21), and *The Nativity* (Luke 2:1-21). Most of these videos would fall in the genre of the music video, which at that time was an innovative and daring way in which to communicate Bible stories. ABS utilized as many media options as were feasible at the time, including VHS videotape, CD-ROM, and an interactive Web site. The videos received much acclaim and won many awards, but they had their detractors as well. As one who has used these videos frequently in college and church-school classrooms, I've never been able to tell whether the negative reviews were in response to the merits of the videos themselves, or in response to the challenging new idea that the Bible could and should be translated from print to electronic media. As easily as we may embrace the new media in our everyday lives, many of us find it hard to imagine anything other than a printed Bible.

In light of the survey of media history above, why was everything I knew about the Bible when I was young, "wrong"?

1. The Bible is a *written*, indeed, a *printed book*.

First of all, the Bible has only been printed for the past 500 years or so, which is only a fraction of the 3000-year history of the Bible. Moreover, large portions of the Bible originated as spoken language, and thus were not even written at first. (Once, the Bible was not a book!) And even when the books of the Bible began to be written, the practices and attitudes of the scribes who produced those manuscripts were much closer to the world of orality than to our own world, in which the printed book still dominates our practices and attitudes. Yes, the books of the Bible were eventually written and even printed, but if we think that is the whole story of the Bible, we will seriously misunderstand much of that story.

---

18. An immense amount of scholarly and artistic collaboration went into the New Media Bible Project, the full story of which is yet to be told. Until it is told, see Paul A. Soukup and Robert Hodgson, eds., *From One Medium to Another: Communicating the Bible through Multimedia* (Kansas City: Sheed & Ward, 1997); Paul A. Soukup, "Transforming the Sacred: The American Bible Society New Media Translation Project," *Journal of Media and Religion* 3 (2004) 101-18.

2. The Bible is a *single book*, completely enclosed between two covers.

The Bible was neither a book nor single when its traditions were in oral form. In fact, at the oral/aural stage, no two tellings of a biblical story would have been the same. Then, at the stage of manuscript communication, no two manuscript copies of a biblical book would have been identical. But this would hardly have mattered much to people who could neither read nor write, which would have been the vast majority of any population before modern times. Long after the biblical books were written, most people would have continued to experience the Bible as ever-changing oral performances, or as translated into other media, such as stained glass, painting, or sculpture.

The literate few who could read books of the Bible probably experienced these books one by one, and not as a complete collection. If a person were lucky, she or he might be able to obtain a manuscript containing the letters of Paul or the four gospels. The books of the Bible were seldom gathered together in one volume before the invention of the printing press.

There is another crucial insight hidden in the title, "The Bible." Our English word *bible* is derived from the Greek, *ta biblia*, which literally means "the little books." This suggests that in the early centuries of Christian history, people knew that their sacred writings were not a single book, but *many* books, indeed, a library of books. To understand the Bible as a library of many different books is to begin to understand that different authors wrote these books, at different times and places, from different perspectives. By contrast, to think that the Bible is a single book is to misunderstand it. Singleness is a lesson taught by print culture, but oral and manuscript cultures teach lessons in fluidity and changeability.

3. The Bible was written *for me*.

This illusion begins to evaporate the instant one realizes and takes seriously that the original languages of the Bible were ancient forms of Hebrew, Aramaic, and Greek.[19] If the biblical authors really had me in mind, they should have used twentieth- or twenty-first-century American English instead. They also would have rejected the

---

19. The illusion also began to fade for me when I realized that my name imprinted with gold letters on the cover of my Bible only meant that my *grandmother* intended that Bible for me, not its ancient authors.

use of the seventeenth-century British English of the King James Bible, if their goal were to get a message through to a Kansas farm boy in the 1950s.

The reality is, of course, that the various books of the Bible were written for other persons, long ago and far away. A good example of this is the letters of the apostle Paul, written to the various Christian communities that he had founded in the Eastern Mediterranean. Often Paul could not be present in person to guide his converts, so he wrote (dictated to a secretary, more precisely) letters to them instead. In reading Paul's letters to the churches in Thessalonica, Galatia, Corinth, Rome, etc., we are quite literally reading someone else's mail. We may learn a great deal from and benefit immensely by reading other people's mail, but we should not fool ourselves into thinking that we were the original, intended recipients. More modestly, people of faith who take the Bible seriously are making a wager that this library of books, written long ago, far away, for other people, can still speak with authority and relevance to us today. That is more than enough.

4. *The contents of the Bible are fixed, unchanging, frozen in amber, forever.*

Only someone reading a printed Bible would think that the Bible is fixed and unchanging. Anyone experiencing the Bible in oral/aural or manuscript form would know otherwise. But even the words on the pages of our printed Bibles are more fluid and changeable than we may realize. Let me offer an example.

Let us imagine a bookstore with a generous selection of Bibles for sale. In the typical American bookstore today, one may have one or two dozen different translations of the Bible from which to choose. If we browse through them, what will we find? The words in the different translations will be—what else?—different! And yet all of these books are all supposed to be "The Bible"? If we come back to that bookstore ten or twenty years later, we will probably find new translations and a few revised editions of the old translations—more evidence that publishers are perfectly capable of producing new versions of the Bible, or changing already existing versions.

In other words, there are different versions of the Bible. These versions contain different words. And many of these versions will undergo revision at some point, which will result in still more changes in language. In short, we do not have to look to oral/aural or manuscript culture to find fluid, changeable wording in our Bibles. It is there in our printed Bibles, if we will open our eyes to see it.

5. The *Bible is "the Word of God."*

Far be it from me to say that this idea is wrong! However, I do want to suggest that, while it may be a truthful statement from the perspective of Christian faith, it is not the whole truth. There is much more that needs to be said.

In surveying the media history of the Bible as we have in this essay, I hope it has become clear that the Bible has a long, rich, and profoundly human history. It was humans who first told the stories now written in our Bibles, and they used their own human languages to do so. It was humans who first wrote the manuscript books of the Bible, and still other humans who creatively copied those manuscripts. Humans produced and printed the many different vernacular translations of the Bible that have appeared since the 1450s. And now those of us living in the Electronic Age face the challenge of how to translate the scriptures into electronic media. The history of the Bible is a profoundly human story from beginning to end.

This is not meant in any way to downplay God's role in the story! According to standard Christian belief, God speaks to humankind in and through the Bible. But to understand the Bible well, we need to understand its media history, and persons of faith need to grasp that God does not only speak through the Bible, but also through the entire history of the Bible. Understanding the 3000-year media history of the Bible helps us better to grasp the true richness and majesty of this marvelous heritage.

Questions

1. When did you first receive a Bible? What lessons, explicit and implicit, did you learn about what the Bible is?

2. What did you learn about the history of the Bible that you did not know before? What did you find most surprising in this history?

3. After reviewing his conclusions, would you agree with Fowler that "everything we know about the Bible is wrong"? Why or why not?

PART I

Story and Performance
in the Ancient World

2

THE STORYTELLING WORLD
OF THE FIRST CENTURY
AND THE GOSPELS

HOLLY E. HEARON

Media Worlds and the Gospels

WE LIVE IN A COMPLEX MEDIA WORLD. ON A DAILY BASIS, we encounter words spoken or written via computers, ipods, cell phones, radios, CD players, televisions, films, theaters, and the printed press, to name but a few. Often we will encounter both spoken and written words in the same moment, sometimes accompanied by visual images, still or streamed. When multi-tasking the encounter is intensified as we find our attention divided between competing voices in sound and image clamoring for our attention. In this complex media world, when we think of the many ways in which we encounter words written or spoken, our first thoughts are likely to be of the various technologies through which the words are mediated. Only secondarily may we consider the persons who give voice to these words.

When we enter the first century C.E. Mediterranean world as it is portrayed in the Gospels, we discover a media world in which the perception and experience of words is the reverse of our own. Rather than associating words with technologies, words are first associated with persons. This is reflected in the Greek where *logoi* ("words") are defined as that which give utterance to the thoughts of the mind.[1] These words are spoken, proclaimed, taught, and debated. They are also written down, most often through dictation to a scribe, then read—not silently, but aloud. Thus even words written begin and end as words spoken. As a consequence, the first question a person in the ancient Mediterranean world might ask concerning a word is not *how* it is communicated but *by whom* is it communicated. Words are inseparable from the people who speak them.

Because of our orientation towards technology, it is natural for us to think of the Gospels primarily as written texts. After all, it is as written texts that the Gospels have been handed down to us. This impression is underscored by two of the Gospel writers who explicitly describe their works as words written. The writer of Luke says that his goal is to write an orderly account of "the events that have been fulfilled among us" (1:1–4), while the writer of John states that "these things are written so that you may come to believe" (20:30; see also 21:24).[2] Both of these statements focus our attention on the written page. The association of the Gospels with the development of the codex (folded pages as opposed to a scroll) further links them in our mind with the production of books. Thus our perceptions of the Gospels tend to be print driven.

Yet as we enter the narrative world of the Gospels, we discover that the Gospels, although written, are oriented towards the spoken word. This can be easily illustrated by looking up the words *write* and *read* in a concordance. The very few references to these words in the four Gospels reveal that the social world portrayed in the Gospels is one in which only a handful of people read or write. Few have need. What is written are legal documents, necessary for the governing of social relations, and the Hebrew Scriptures. Yet the latter are nearly always described as texts read aloud so that they are heard. Thus the vast majority of people negotiate the world exclusively through words spoken and heard rather than words written and read. This invites us to make a perceptual shift when we think of the Gospels: to envision them not in terms of written texts, but to think of them as words spoken, as stories told.

---

1. Frederick William Danker, ed *A Greek-English Lexicon of the New Testament and Other Early Christian Literature,* 3rd ed. (Chicago: University of Chicago Press, 2000) 599. A second word, *rhēma,* refers to that which is said, such as a word, saying, or statement (ibid., 905).

2. All quotations of the New Testament are taken from the New Revised Standard Version.

The two Gospel writers mentioned above help us to make this transition. The writer of Luke tells us in the prologue to the Gospel that he (or she) is drawing on traditional stories that have been "handed on" by those who had firsthand knowledge of the events (1:1–4).[3] The writer of John concludes that Gospel by stating that, in addition to the things written here, there are many other things that Jesus did that have not been written down (20:30; 21:25). Both of these statements indicate that the written texts represented by these Gospels are, so to speak, just the tip of the iceberg. There are many stories about Jesus in circulation. Some have been woven together to create the written Gospel narratives, but others are held in memory and exist only when spoken by a storyteller.

Within the Gospels we have at least two examples of these stories that are in circulation, signaled by their resistance to being assigned a fixed place in the written text. The story of 'the woman charged with adultery' is printed in most Bibles at John 7:53—8:11. Yet other early manuscripts of the Gospels place the story after John 7:36, others after Luke 21:28 or Luke 24:53, while still others omit the story altogether. The multiple manuscript homes assigned to this story suggests that it is one of the stories about Jesus that is circulating orally. Scribes who knew the story assigned it to one or another Gospel, although it does not appear to have belonged to the original narrative of either Luke or John. A second example is the story of the miraculous catch of fish. This story is recorded in John 21:4–8 as a post-resurrection appearance of Jesus to Peter and other disciples. A remarkably similar story appears in Luke 5:1–11, but as a pre-resurrection story in which Jesus calls Peter to follow him. Assuming that both writers are drawing on a known tradition, the radically different setting of the story in each Gospel suggests that the story was adapted by oral storytellers, and that these different tellings were recorded by the writers of Luke and John.[4]

---

3. Loveday Alexander suggests that "eyewitnesses" are not forensic witnesses such as would be called on in a court of law, but those who have intimate knowledge of the events; *The Preface to Luke's Gospel: Literary Convention and Social Context in Luke 1.1–4 and Acts 1.1*, Society for the Study of the New Testament Monograph Series 78 (Cambridge: Cambridge University Press, 1993) 120–22.

4. Two other examples may be found in the multiple versions of the anointing of Jesus in Mark, Luke, and John, and the post-resurrection appearance to Mary Magdalene, told in Matt 28:9–10 and John 20:1–20.

Storytelling in the Ancient Mediterranean World

In order to envision the Gospels as words spoken rather than words written, we need to explore the storytelling world of the first century C.E. This is a more challenging enterprise than may appear on the surface. We know that storytelling took place; the difficulty is that it was such a common activity that few writers in the ancient world commented upon it. Since it was an activity with which everyone was familiar there was no need to describe who told stories to whom, what kind of stories were told, and in what contexts storytelling took place. Everyone knew! A difficulty for us is that, because storytelling is also a common activity in our world, we may assume that we know more about storytelling in the ancient world than we, in fact, do know. Studies by folklorists today are careful to observe that, although storytelling seems to be found in every culture, every culture has its own rules that govern practices of storytelling. We need to exercise the same caution when we approach the ancient world. In order to understand the storytelling practices that contributed to the emergence and circulation of the Gospels we need to look at what ancient writers say about storytelling and how they describe actual instances of storytelling. Remember, there is no treatise on storytelling available to us: everything we can know must be gleaned from circumstantial evidence. It is a little like putting together a jigsaw puzzle, except that in this case we have no photo to tell us what the finished picture should look like.

Carrying forward the metaphor of a jigsaw puzzle, let us begin to look at some of the pieces that belong to this puzzle. In one pile we can gather together those pieces that offer opinions about storytelling. We do well to keep in mind that these are expressed by writers in the ancient world who belong to the literary and social elite. These writers tend to assign love of stories to the uneducated, describing them as children, whose faculties of reasoning have not yet fully developed.[5] Women also are described as especially fond of stories. Like children, women were thought to be particularly susceptible to belief in the fantastical; hence when a writer wants to cast doubt on the credibility of a story they describe it as "an old wives' tale." The elderly, too, are said to be susceptible to "love of romance stories."[6] Notice who is missing from this collection of puzzle pieces: educated, elite men. This should alert us to the care with which we

5. Strabo *Geography* 1.2.8.

6. Longinus *On the Sublime* 9.11.

need to read our sources. Despite the opinions expressed by many elite male writers towards those who enjoy stories, we also find evidence that storytelling took place among these elite men. Pliny the Younger, for example, evokes the cry of a storyteller when writing to a friend, "Have your copper ready and hear a first-rate story, or rather stories, for the new one has reminded me of others and it doesn't matter which I tell first."[7] The emperor Augustus is also reported to have called for a storyteller when he could not sleep.[8] Thus, despite popular stereotypes, we know that stories were told and enjoyed by people at all levels of society.

Professional Storytellers

Other pieces of the puzzle point to the presence of professional storytellers in the first century Mediterranean world. In addition to the storyteller whom Augustus called in when he could not sleep, the emperor was known to employ professional storytellers to entertain his guests when he held a feast.[9] Another writer, Dio Chrysostom, comments on the sight of storytellers hawking their tales as he strolled through the Hippodrome.[10] The popularity of storytelling as a form of public entertainment is suggested also by the writer Apuleius who adopts the role of a professional storyteller in his novel *The Golden Ass:* "In this Milesian tale I shall string together diverse stories and delight your kindly ears with a pleasant history, if you will not scorn to look upon this Egyptian paper written with a ready pen of Nile reeds—stories of men's forms and fortunes transformed."[11] Individuals who served some kind of formal role within religious groups could also function in the capacity of professional storytellers. Stories about the gods were told by priests, and related in hymns, dramas, and visual images.[12] Numerous stories also were told by and about the rabbis. Some of these stories bear close resemblance to stories that we encounter in the Gospels: for example, a story in which the rabbis

---

7. Pliny *Letters* 2.20.1 (Radice, LCL).

8. Seutonius *Augustus* 78.2.

9. Ibid., 74, 78.

10. Dio Chrysostum *Orations* 20.10.

11 Apuleius *The Golden Ass* 1.1 (Adlington, LCL).

12. Alexander Scobie, "Storytellers, Storytelling, and the Novel in Graeco-Roman Antiquity," *Rheineisches Museum für Philologie* 122 (1979) 241; Clement of Alexandria *Exhortation to the Greeks* 1.2.

discuss who is the greatest, or another in which there is a miraculous provision of bread.[13] Of course, Jesus might also be included in this group, since he is portrayed in three of the Gospels (Mark, Matthew, and Luke) as a teller of parables. It is important to note that these religious persons are never specifically called storytellers; rather, their role as storytellers is indicated by their function (bearers of the tradition) and activities (e.g., stories about rabbis telling stories).

This is important to keep in mind when we consider the question of storytellers within the early Christian movement. No one in the New Testament is called a 'storyteller,' nor does storytelling occur in lists of roles and functions within early Christian communities (see, e.g., Rom 12:4–8; 1 Cor 12:8–10; 1 Tim 3:1–13; 5:17–22). While some have suggested that storytelling would be among the functions of the apostles (the speeches assigned to Peter in Acts, for example, could be seen as a kind of storytelling), they are never described *specifically* as storytellers. Yet the absence of vocabulary related to the *role* of storyteller tells only half the story, as it were. There are numerous places where we are alerted that stories are being told. For example, in Mark 1:45, a leper who has been healed by Jesus "spreads the word" of this amazing event while in Mark 5:27 the woman with a flow of blood approaches Jesus because she has heard stories about his ability to heal. Stories are circulating; however, they are being told not by professional storytellers but by people whose lives have been touched by Jesus and by people who are amazed at the things that they are hearing about Jesus. Thus the first stories that arise about Jesus emerge among informal storytellers.

Later Christian texts that offer evidence of storytelling support this impression. Papias, who lived during the first half of the second century, recounts stories of miraculous healings that he had heard from the daughters of Philip, who were prophets.[14] We may not associate storytelling with prophecy, but prophets could function as storytellers. The prophet Nathan, for example, tells a story to David to point out the wrong he has committed in having Uriah killed in order to cover up his seduction of Bathsheba (2 Sam 12:1–15). Whether the daughters of Philip are telling these stories in their prophetic role, however, is not clear. Papias may identify his source because these women were known to those to whom

---

13. *b. Qiddushin.*32b; *b. Ta'anit* 24b–25a.

14. Eusebius *Eccesiastical History* 3.39; 3.31.

he is writing, or because he wants to assure his readers that these stories come from a reliable source (or possibly both). Clement of Alexandria (second half of the first century) tells a "true story" of John the apostle which he says "had been handed down and preserved in memory."[15] It is striking that, although Clement emphasizes that the story has been "handed down" and "preserved," he does not mention from whom he received the story. This indicates two things: firstly, that it is the story, rather than the storyteller, that is of primary interest to Clement; and secondly, that Clement does not view the telling of the story as belonging to the private domain of particular individuals. Nonetheless, the fact that the story has been "preserved in memory" and "handed down" indicates that it is a story that is significant for these early Christians. There can be no doubt, then, that stories are being told, remembered, and retold. But who are the storytellers? While there may be formal or professional storytellers within the early Christian movement, the weight of the evidence suggests that storytelling is not the domain of a few individuals, but is an informal activity that is engaged in by many people.

Informal Storytellers

As we continue to sort our puzzle pieces we discover that both men and women functioned as informal storytellers. Consistent with the stereotypes mentioned earlier, old women are often portrayed as storytellers in dubious settings, passing along "old wives' tales." In Xenophon's *An Ephesian Tale,* an old woman at an inn tells a story about the untimely death of a young woman to a drinking party of men, while in Apuleius' *The Golden Ass,* an old woman who serves a band of thieves tells a story to comfort a young woman who has been kidnapped by the bandits.[16] The writer of 1 Timothy draws on this reputation when he accuses widows of being gossips and busybodies who are "gadding about from house to house" (5:13). It is likely that the widows are telling stories of which the author does not approve. It is not only old women, however, who are tellers of tales. Old men, too, are noted for spinning yarns about past exploits. In another ancient novel, *Daphnis and Chloe,* Longus describes how old men "when they are a little whittled with wine, they had various discourses and chats amongst them; how bravely in their youth they

---

15. Clement of Alexandria *Rich Man* 42.1.2 (Butterworth, LCL).
16. Xenophon *An Ephesian Tale* 3.9; Apuleius *The Golden Ass* 4.27—6.24.

had administered the pasturing of their flocks and herds, how in their time they had escaped very many invasions and inroads of pirates and thieves."[17] While these descriptions are certainly entertaining, and probably bear some resemblance to reality, we would do well not to cast all old women and men as tellers of fanciful tales. Respect for elders was a social value in the ancient world. So the writer of 1 Timothy also admonishes readers to "not speak harshly to an older man, but speak to him as to a father . . . to older women as mothers" (5:1–2). In keeping with this social value, Lelex, a character in Ovid's *Metamorphoses* who is described as a man "ripe in mind and years," tells a story in order to admonish a younger man for his attitude.[18] Older men and women could also tell stories as a way of offering guidance to younger men and women.

Women as Storytellers

As age decreases, the evidence points to some distinctions between women and men as storytellers and the contexts in which they tell stories, inviting us to sort these puzzle pieces into two piles. Women are described telling stories to children in their roles as mothers and nurses. These stories are anything but harmless tales. Plato recognized the power of stories to shape the minds and characters of young children and suggested that censorship should be applied so that "the first stories [the children] hear should be so composed as to bring the fairest lessons of virtue to their ears."[19] We encounter a similar attitude today when parents use a blocking device to prevent their children from viewing certain television programs or Web sites. Particularly interesting is the recognition that it is in the home, and from mothers and nurses, that children first are taught stories about the gods.[20] Thus, although the religion of the household is most often determined by the father in the patriarchal household of antiquity, it is women who first provide religious instruction to their children through the stories that they tell. We can assume that this pattern would be no different in households in the early Christian movement. The description of Timothy inheriting his faith from his grandmother Lois and his mother, Eunice, points in this direction (2 Tim 1:5).

---

17. Longus *Daphnis and Chloe* 2.32 (Thornley, LCL).

18. Ovid *Metamorphoses* 8.612 (Miller, LCL).

19. Plato *Republic* 378.E.1 (Shorey, LCL).

20. Plato *Laws* 10.887D; Plutarch *Theseus* 23.3.

Women are not confined to telling stories to children, however. They also tell stories to each other. In Ovid's *Metamorphoses* a group of sisters tell stories to one another to pass the time as they work: "the daughters of Minyas . . . ply their household tasks, spinning wool, thumbing the turning threads, or keep close to the loom, and press their maidens work. Then one of them, drawing the thread the while with deft thumb says: '. . . to beguile the tedious hours, let us take turns in telling stories while all the others listen.'"[21] Although women would have spent many hours spinning and weaving, inscriptions from the ancient world reveal that women were involved in many trades and occupations, for example, as a farmer, a fish-monger, or a dealer in grains and vegetables.[22] In these contexts, as well, women would have had occasion to tell stories to one another, or exchange stories with customers in the course of a day. Other examples of women telling stories include a mother-in-law and daughter-in-law exchanging stories about giving birth, and one woman telling another of being forced to accept the amorous advances of an unwanted suitor.[23] These stories out of women's lives would have provided an informal way to pass on advice or offer comfort and encouragement (see the chapter by Joanna Dewey for an example of this). A number of stories from the Gospels serve as illustrations here: for example, the story of Syrophoenician woman who begs Jesus to heal her daughter (Mark 7:24–30), the mother-in-law of Peter who is healed (see especially Matthew's version in 8:14–15), or the grateful woman who anoints Jesus' feet (Luke 7:36–50).

Men as Storytellers

Men, no less than women, also are described telling stories to one an-other. Very often, these stories are about their own adventures or mis-adventures: stories of ill-fated love or a marriage destroyed, of victory in battle or being rescued from near death, or, in the case of thieves, of robberies, successful and unsuccessful. They also pass along stories about other men (less often about women) as well as stories about the gods. When we consider the Gospels, we find a large number of stories that

21. Ovid, *Metamorphoses* 4.32–42 (Miller, LCL).

22. *CIL* VI.3482 (=*ILS* 7459.L), *CIL* VI.9801 (=*ILS* 7500), and *CIL* VI.9683 (= *ILS* 7488), cited in Mary Lefkowitz and Maureen Fant, eds. *Women's Life in Greece and Rome* (Baltimore: Johns Hopkins University Press, 1992) 209, 223, 224.

23. Ovid *Metamorphoses* 9.285–391; 13.738–898.

focus on the experience of men: arguments over who is greatest that arise among those who travel with Jesus, for example (Mark 9:33–37); a rich man who asks Jesus what he must do to inherit eternal life (Mark 10:17–22); a blind man who is healed (Mark 10:46–52). While women tend to be described telling stories within the context of the home, men more often tell their stories in public settings: over a meal at an inn or at a banquet, at a religious festival, or while traveling. Particularly striking here is the way Jesus is described as a man on a journey, telling stories to whomever will listen. Finally, just as women exchange stories so, too, men are frequently described engaging in reciprocal storytelling with first one and then another telling a story. In some instances this exchange becomes a kind of a competition, with one trying to best the other. In the novel *Leucippe and Clitophon,* for example, one character warns another not to underestimate the ability of a gnat to torment an elephant; the other retorts with a story about the gnat becoming caught in a spider web.[24] This is not unlike the kind of exchanges Jesus enters into with religious leaders (see, e.g., Matt 21:23–40).

Men and Women Telling Stories Together

Although men and women's storytelling tends to take place within 'gender spheres' there are occasions when men and women tell stories together. Older women, perhaps by virtue of their age and experience, seem to have the freedom to address groups with only men or groups composed of both men and women. In addition, mixed gender storytelling takes place within family groups and over meals where the individuals are known to one another. So, for example, a mother, father, daughter, and the daughter's beloved tell stories over a meal in *Daphnis and Chloe.*[25] This is significant for our consideration of storytelling in early Christian movements for two reasons: First, members of early Christian movements recognized each other as brothers and sisters in Christ (so, e.g., Rom 1:13;

---

24. Achilles Tatius *Leucippe and Clitophon* 2.21.5.4.

25. Longus *Daphnis and Chloe* 3.9. In a study of contemporary folklore, Karen Baldwin observes that in private settings, men and women often collaborate in telling stories, with the women describing the context for and correcting the men's tales. Karen Baldwin, "Woof! A Word on Women's Roles in Family Storytelling," in Jordan and Kalčik [note caron over c], eds. *Women's Folklore, Women's Culture* (Philadelphia: University of Pennsylvania Press, 1985) 155.

1 Cor 1:10).[26] Thus they understood themselves to be related to one another as a family or fictive kinship group. Second, the earliest Christian gatherings are believed to have been in house churches.[27] Since women have always been storytellers in the home, and because the men and women gathered there understood themselves to be an extended family, it is probable that both men and women were active storytellers in early Christian communities. A likely setting for such storytelling would be a meal, such as the one described in 1 Corinthians 11:17–22. Although it is possible that a single storyteller was invited to speak, it is also possible that stories were exchanged, as one person built upon the story of another. This would be consistent with the storytelling practices described by our sources.

Functions of Storytelling

We have focused so far on gathering pieces of the puzzle that describe who told stories to whom, and where. Another important piece of the puzzle is the question of why stories were told. Of course, the most obvious reasons were to pass the time and provide entertainment. There were no televisions, radios, or movie theaters, much less computers or ipods. Stories provided a way to escape the tedium of the task or the boredom of the day, as the writer of *The Golden Ass* observes, commenting that a story told by Aristomenes shortened a long and weary journey.[28]

In addition to entertainment, stories could also serve an educational function. According to Theon, writing in his manual of educational exercises, *mythoi* (stories) were also called *ainoi* (stories with a moral) because they provided advice.[29] Plato recognized that the entertaining quality of stories made learning more palatable—as when a professor deviates from scripted notes and launches into a story from her own experience by way

26. In Greek, the word often translated "brothers and sisters" is *adelphoi*. Some translations render this "brothers." However, Greek is a gendered language; the masculine plural is used when referring to a group of both men and women.

27. Elisabeth Schüssler Fiorenza, *In Memory of Her: A Feminist Theological Reconstruction of Christian Origins* (New York: Crossroad, 1984) 176.

28. Apuleius, *The Gold Ass* 1.20.

29. Theon, *Progymnasmata* 73, in George A. Kennedy, trans., *Progymnasmata: Greek Textbooks of Prose Composition and Rhetoric,* Writings from the Greco-Roman World 10 (Atlanta: Society of Biblical Literature, 2003) 24.

of example.[30] Stories, therefore, provided an effective way to offer guidance, instill values, and shape attitudes. Pliny illustrates this function of stories in his letter to Junius Avitus. In his letter, Pliny tells a story about dining with a man who served the best dishes to himself, reserving the cheaper food for his company. "The point of this story," Pliny concludes, "is to prevent a promising young man like yourself from being taken in by this extravagance under the guise of economy."[31]

The telling of stories to instill values and shape attitudes not only served an educational function—i.e. the teaching of moral lessons; it also served to shape identity. Strabo comments, "It is fondness for tales, then, that induces children to give their attention to narratives and more and more to take part in them."[32] Strabo's comment points to an important dimension of stories: Stories invite listeners to enter the world of the story, to identify with the characters, and be transformed with them or by them (see the essays by Rhoads, Ruge-Jones, Swanson, and Steussy). A wonderful illustration of this is found in the novel *Leucippe and Clitophon*. Clitophon, in a moment of despair, recalls the story of Niobe—the Queen of Thebes whose fourteen children were slaughtered in a single moment—and recognizes in Niobe's grief his own.[33] This point of identification fosters empathy with others who suffer and also provides Clitophon with a model of how to behave in his state of grief. The story of the Good Samaritan in the Gospel of Luke (10:25–37) is narrated precisely for the purpose of inviting such identification ("Go and do likewise"; v. 37). This potential for identification is one of the most powerful and dynamic functions of story.[34]

It is precisely because stories cultivate a sense of shared identity that they are also effective tools for the purposes of persuasion. Strabo remarks, "For in dealing with a crowd of women, at least, or with any promiscuous mob, a philosopher cannot influence them by reason or exhort them to reverence, piety and faith . . . this cannot be aroused without myths (*mythoi*) and marvels."[35] Where reason and argument fail, stories prevail.

30. Plato, *Laws* 840C.1; *Republic* 378.E.1.

31. Pliny, *Letters* 2.6.6 (Radice, LCL).

32. Strabo, *Geography* 1.2.8 (Jones, LCL).

33. Achilles Tatius *Leucippe and Clitophon* 3.15.6.2.

34. Identification does not always mean "go and do likewise"; sometimes identification is intended to warn hearers against a course of action or behavior.

35. Strabo *Geography* 1.2.8 (Jones, LCL).

The Roman historian Dio Cassius relates how a mob of debtors took possession of a hill; in an effort to defuse the situation, Agrippa addressed the mob with a story about how the various parts of the body are mutually dependent on one another in order to illustrate how the abundance of the rich also supports the poor.[36] The story had the desired affect and the mob dispersed. Paul, coincidentally, uses this same image to persuade the Corinthians that the diverse members of the community are all necessary for the well-being of the body of faith (1 Cor 12:12–26).

Stories could also be used to divide a crowd by pitting the claims of one person or group against those of another. The writer of 2 Peter, for example, declares, "we did not follow cleverly devised stories" (1:16), implying that the stories he has shared with them are true, in contrast to those told by others. When reading the Gospels, it is possible at some points to feel the tension of competing stories not far beneath the surface. For example, in the Gospel of Luke, the disciples on the road to Emmaus are the first to see the risen Jesus. Yet when they arrive in Jerusalem and announce to the disciples there that Jesus has appeared to them, they are told that this is old news because Jesus has appeared (already) to Simon. This appearance to Simon (Peter) coincides with Paul's report that Jesus appeared first to Cephas (Peter, 1 Cor 15:5). However, in the Gospels of Matthew and John, Jesus appears first to Mary Magdalene. Whose story should the community of believers accept? The answer to that question may reside in who it is that is telling the story and whether or not we believe, not the story, but him—or her.

Piecing Together the Picture

As we begin to fit together our various piles of jigsaw puzzle pieces, the picture that emerges is crowded with people. Storytelling is fundamentally a social activity. Stories written require no more than a reader and a text. In the ancient world, stories spoken were dependent upon at least two people being in the same place at the same time. How the story was told and how it was heard was shaped by the relationships among the people present and the circumstances that drew them together. Although certain settings and occasions gave rise to storytelling (meals, shared tasks, journeys), it was the presence of people and the intersection of their lives

36. Dio Cassius *Roman History* 4.1.10.9.

that called forth the story. Setting, therefore, was less about place than it was about group: who was present, what kind of story was called for by the particular group that was present, and what social needs were to be addressed by the story. The Gospels emerged in just such a storytelling context. What we experience as a written word was experienced by the earliest Christians as a spoken word, a story told, by one person to another as they shared a meal, spun wool, or undertook a journey together—long before the stories were ever written down.

Our picture also reveals a variety of groups in which storytelling took place, and points to a variety of storytellers. Although certain individuals may have been sought out because of their ability as a storyteller, or because of the status they enjoyed within the community, there is no evidence to suggest that storytelling was restricted or assigned. Rather it was an activity that many people participated in, both men and women. When we encounter the Gospels as written texts, we tend to think of a single voice behind the texts: either the voice of God or the voice of the New Testament or the voice of the Bible. Even when we read the texts aloud, this is the voice we give voice to. In the storytelling world of the first century, the stories of the Gospels were associated with many voices. Some of these voices were old, some were polished and practiced, while others were still learning how to find the right words. But the stories they told were told in their own voice and in their own way. They told the stories to people whom, for the most part, they knew and whose stories they would hear in return. The stories could not be separated from the people who told them.

Often they told stories for the purposes of sheer entertainment. Yet even these stories could become a means of building a shared identity within a group. The stories created a space that they could inhabit together and in which they found themselves bound together by a common experience. On the other hand, stories could be told also to divide a group or introduce tension by challenging the hearers to choose one story over another. Either way, storytelling was a dynamic social activity defined by the intersection of the person who told the story, the person or group who heard it, and the effect it created. When we think of the Gospels, we are likely to think of them in terms of one dimension: as stories written to promote faith. When we hear them as stories told, we become alert to the social impact of the Gospel stories. Moreover, we become aware that some Gospel stories stand in tension with other Gospel stories, pointing to social tensions that existed between one and another group within the early Christian movement. This invites us to consider whose interests are represented by these stories, and whose are not. And when the Gospels are finally translated from spoken word into written word, whose stories are recorded, and whose stories are forgotten as memory of them dies with the persons who told them?

Questions

1. What are some of the different ways you encounter storytelling? In what media does this storytelling occur? Who tells the stories, and what kind of stories do they tell?

2. Who tells stories in the ancient world and in what settings? In what ways is storytelling in the ancient world similar to or different from storytelling today?

3. Does the suggestion that the Gospels arose from oral storytelling in the ancient world alter the way you think about the Bible? What questions does it raise about the nature of the Bible and the purposes it serves?

3

WOMEN ON THE WAY

A Reconstruction of Late First-Century Women's Storytelling

Joanna Dewey

Introduction

FOR MORE THAN FIFTEEN YEARS, I HAVE BEEN PERFORMING for classes, church groups, and worship services, "Women on the Way." It is a version of the Gospel of Mark as I imagine a late first-century Gentile woman might have told the story; it is "Artemisia's" rendition of traditions she has heard, going back to Ruth, a disciple of Jesus. Two scholarly concerns led me to develop this performance: first, the recognition of the oral medium in the ancient Mediterranean world and, in particular, the importance of oral storytelling in the spread of early Christianity; and second, the need to integrate feminist scholarship about the women around Jesus and in early Christianity into my teaching of the New Testament. So I decided to tell the plot of Mark's Gospel about discipleship as a woman storyteller might have told it to Gentiles some seventy years after the first Easter. I use all my knowledge of oral storytelling techniques and first-century women's lives to inform my story.

The first century media world is well covered in other articles in this volume, and the importance of story has been dealt with in Holly Hearon's article. Perhaps, overall, 5 percent of people were to some degree literate, a higher percentage in urban than rural areas and a higher percentage among men than among women. Except among the few elite males, nonliteracy was neither a shame nor an inconvenience. Information was conveyed orally, often shaped as stories, which are easy to remember. Women participated actively in storytelling, telling stories to children, to women, and to mixed groups of men and women.[1] So early followers of Jesus heard and told brief stories about Jesus and lengthier narratives about his life and death. They did not read them or customarily hear them read aloud from a manuscript. Even after the composition of the Gospel of Mark in writing around 70 C.E., the Gospel was told and retold, often independently of any contact with a manuscript.[2] Today, for us, Scripture is a fixed printed text. The way to give students a feel for story—for oral performance—as the basic medium of early Christianity is to model it, by telling a story.

The story that I offer here is not intended as an eyewitness account but rather as a story shaped over decades of being told and re-told to different audiences. My storyteller is a woman I name Artemisia. She lives outside of Ephesus on the coast of Asia Minor (modern day Turkey). She tells a story that has been passed on to her over time. The story in its beginning goes back to a woman named Ruth; therefore Artemisia calls this story the Gospel of Ruth.

We are not accustomed to thinking of women as disciples of Jesus or as early Christian leaders. That is because the New Testament, like most literature, consists of androcentric texts. Androcentrism is a mind-set or attitude in which the male represents the human norm; the female is embedded in the male, which renders her secondary and generally invisible. She is considered a deviation from this human (male) norm and of inferior value. The female is only mentioned when she is a problem to the man, she is very exceptional, or otherwise necessary to the story.[3] Think of the story of the ten lepers in Luke 17:11–19: do you think of ten men or a mixed group? Or think of the two on the road to Emmaus in Luke 24:13–35: do you think of the two disciples as two men or, which is more

---

1. Joanna Dewey, "From Storytelling to Written Text: The Loss of Early Christian Women's Voices," *Biblical Theology Bulletin* 26 (1996) 71–78; Holly E. Hearon, *The Mary Magdalene Tradition: Witness and Counter-Witness in Early Christian Communities* (Collegeville, MN: Liturgical, 2004).

2. Joanna Dewey, "Mark—A Really Good Oral Story: Is That Why the Gospel of Mark Survived?" *Journal of Biblical Literature* 123 (2004) 495–507.

3. This definition is based on the work of Elisabeth Schüssler Fiorenza, *In Memory of Her: A Feminist Theological Reconstruction of Christian Origins* (New York: Crossroad, 1983). For more information about the women around Jesus and as early Christian leaders, see *In Memory of Her*, 105–241.

probable, a husband and wife? Mark has composed an androcentric text: he only mentions the women disciples fifteen verses before the end of his narrative, because he now needs them as characters in his plot. At the arrest of Jesus, Mark has portrayed the male disciples all running away. With the male disciples now absent from the story, Mark mentions for the first time that there have been women accompanying Jesus in Galilee and on the way to Jerusalem. The women have been there all along. It is these women disciples who witness the crucifixion, observe the burial, and discover the empty tomb (Mark 15:40–41, 47; 16:1–8). The male disciples are not heard from again in Mark's narrative. In my performance, I attempt to remove the androcentric lens and portray the women as present throughout the story.

The New Testament provides abundant evidence of women around Jesus and of women as leaders in early Christian churches. Women are members of Jesus' discipleship community throughout his ministry (Mark 15:40–41; Matt 27:55–56; Luke 8:1–3). In all four gospels, it is the women who discover the empty tomb. In Matthew and John, they are the first witnesses of the resurrection.[4] In the Gospel of John, it is Martha, not Peter, who recognizes Jesus as the Christ (John 11:27; cf. Mark 8:29; Matt 16:16; Luke 9:20).[5] Furthermore, there are women who are early Christian leaders.[6] Women are traveling missionaries and leaders of house churches. There is no title–minister (deacon), apostle, coworker–that Paul applies to a man that he does not also apply to a woman.[7] Furthermore, in all of Paul's undisputed letters, of the forty leaders named, sixteen of them or forty per cent are women.

We can assume, therefore, that Mark's first audiences and Christians throughout the first centuries of the Common Era would have known women as Christian leaders, and would have known stories about women and by women who followed Jesus. When those first audiences imagined

---

4. Mark has no resurrection appearances. In the longer ending added to Mark, women again are the first witnesses of the resurrection.

5. For other prominent women around Jesus, see also Mark 7:24–30; 14:3–9; Matt 26:6–13; John 4:1–42.

6. For details, see Margaret Y. MacDonald, "Reading Real Women through the Undisputed Letters of Paul," in Ross Shepard Kraemer and Mary Rose D'Angelo, eds., *Women and Christian Origins* (New York: Oxford University Press, 1999) 199–220.

7. For Junia as an apostle, see Rom 16:7. See Eldon Jay Epp, *Junia: The First Woman Apostle* (Minneapolis: Fortress, 2005).

the world of Jesus, they would have pictured women as well as men ac-companying Jesus. Consequently when they heard Mark's androcentric gospel, presenting only men among the inner circle around Jesus until after the crucifixion, these audiences would likely have placed Mark's story into their own picture of Jesus' world, and imagined women among the inner circle around Jesus. After centuries of experiencing only the androcentric gospels, we need to broaden our imaginations so that we, too, can remember these women.

Of course, we have no oral stories from women that were recorded in writing in the New Testament. We can only imagine how women told stories in early Christianity. We do know, however, about storytelling and about the roles of women. What follows is how I imagine Artemisia in the late first-century might have told the story about Jesus from the perspective of Jesus' disciple, Ruth.

Script for Performance

Introduction of Artemisia to a Contemporary Audience

We welcome Artemisia here today. She is visiting us from Ephesus where she lived about seventy years after Jesus' execution in Jerusalem. She will tell us the story of Ruth. She heard the story from her aunt Philia who heard it from her Jewish woman friend, who heard it from others, the tradition going all the way back to Ruth. Welcome.

Artemisia's Narrative

I invite you to imagine yourselves living in the last years of the first century. You are living in a small coastal fishing village, say, on the coast of Turkey, just outside Ephesus. It's late in the day; it's a warm, balmy evening.

You have finished your day's labor. You women have baked and cooked and cared for the children. The poorer among you–and that's most of you–have returned from working in the houses and fields of the wealthy on the nearby estates, cooking, cleaning, and caring for other people's children. You have returned to feed the men who have come in from the fishing boats, and from cleaning their nets, some from working as day laborers in nearby fields. And now, finally, you women have fed your families; the day's work is done.

It's not yet time for bed, and your homes are small and dark and stuffy, so you go out to gather in the village square. The men and the boys take up most of the square, talking about whatever it is that men talk about when they are together. And the women and girls, and all the children under say nine or ten, you are all crowded in one corner of the square, your corner, near the path to the community baking ovens, gossiping about the day, about how hard you've worked, and about what the children have done and said.

And Chloris and I walk into the square and join the women. We've walked over from the outskirts of Ephesus, where we live. I've come to visit my daughter, Tatia, and visit my grandchildren.

Pretty soon, the women and girls begin badgering me to tell them a story. There's not much to do in the evenings, no outside entertainment. We don't know how to read; we don't need to. Only the village scribe knows how to read and write a bit and even he has to fish to earn enough to live. So that's why we tell stories, and good storytellers are in demand.

Now, I pride myself on my storytelling. Wherever I go, the women gather to hear me tell stories. I have a reputation throughout the whole region. People know me as Artemisia, the teller of tales. So tonight, in the village gathering, the girls clamor: tell us the gospel according to Ruth, tell us Ruth's story.

The men even creep over to the outskirts of our group to hear my story. Of course, men don't spend time chatting with women in public–they think it's shameful. But I'm a good storyteller, better than any they have tonight. Besides, Tatia's husband is very fond of me, and he's one of the chief men of the village. So, as he comes to listen, the other men–some of them anyway–come over too. Well, I began Ruth's story.

The beginning of the gospel of Jesus Christ, Son of God. Hannah and I were at our fish place in the village market on market day selling and bartering to whoever came by. And Jesus came into the village, proclaiming, "The realm of God is at hand. Turn and trust the good news"–he proclaimed God's realm, not Caesar's, not the kingdom of Rome. And we were watching, Hannah and I, as Jesus went down by the lake. Simon and Andrew were there cleaning their nets. And Jesus looked at them, and we could see he said something, and immediately Simon and Andrew got up and left their nets and followed him. They just left their nets. Some people from the neighboring boat came over and pulled their nets the rest of the way up on shore, but Simon and Andrew just left their nets and walked off following Jesus.

And immediately Jesus came past Hannah and me. And he looked at us, and he said, "Come after me and be fishers of people." So Hannah and I, we left our place and we followed after him. It was the end of the day, most of the fish were sold, but we just left our place, and followed him.

As soon as it was sundown, as soon as the Sabbath started, we all went to the synagogue assembly. Thaddeus, the man with the demon, he was there disrupting the worship again. I've always felt sorry for his family, they try to care for him, they try to keep him under control. But you can't control a demon. And Jesus, Jesus commanded the demon, he told it to *shut up!* And the demon came out of him and Thaddeus was in his right mind. We've never seen anything like this!

And immediately we went to Martha's house, and Martha's mother was sick with a fever, and Jesus went to her, and took her hand and raised her up. And you know, she started ministering to us. And we began traveling through the villages. People kept crowding around Jesus, bringing their sick, and Jesus taught them and healed them all and cast out the demons. Sometimes scribes came and challenged him about what he was doing, healing on the Sabbath, or eating with tax collectors and sinners, but he always had a good comeback. I really love how he always has a quick retort. A little scary too, it can be risky to challenge the authorities. As we went through the villages, the crowds around Jesus got bigger and bigger.

Then Jesus chose some of us to be with him. Out of the huge crowds following, he named a group of us to be with him, to preach and to heal. He named Hannah and me and some other women; he named Simon Peter and Andrew and some of the men.

And right away Jesus began to teach us. One day when we were indoors, Jesus' mother came with his brothers to fetch him, to take him home where he belonged. He didn't go. Rather he told us that whoever does the will of God is his mother, brother, and sister. He taught us, we are truly his relatives, his kin, we are a new family together.

And crowds followed us wherever we went. So one day Jesus got in a boat on the shore of the lake so he wouldn't get crushed by the crowd, and he taught them from the boat. He told parables, these little stories, about the seed and the sower, and all these types of soil, about the farmer who planted seed and waited and waited, and about the mustard seed that grew into a great big bush. And we asked them what the stories meant.

We asked him to explain them to us, and he told us, "To you has been given the mystery of God's realm," but then he said, "Why don't you understand this story? If you can't get this story, how will you understand all the other stories?" You know, sometimes I wish Jesus had a bit more patience, that he would explain things more; I heard James and John say the same thing. Indeed the men with us don't seem to understand any better than we do—sometimes I think they don't even get it as well.

And immediately Jesus had us get into the boat with him. Now, I don't like boats. To tell you the truth, I'm terrified of the water—I don't know how to swim. But we were all getting in the boat, so I got into the boat. And it was worse than I ever could have imagined. A storm came up, waves and wind, and we were being drenched with the spray. I was sure we'd all drown. And Jesus, Jesus was just sitting on a cushion at the back of the boat, asleep. How could he sleep through this? Even the fishermen were terrified. But there he was, sleeping through it. So we woke him up.

And you know what he did: he got up and he told the wind and the sea to *shut up*, just as he had told the demon, and they did. Immediately the sea was calm, and the wind died right down. Who is this, that even the wind and the sea obey him?

And we continued to go about the villages. And Jairus, the synagogue leader, came and begged Jesus to come and heal his daughter. We set off, all of us, a big crowd, after Jairus. And suddenly Jesus stopped and said, "Who touched me?" And we looked at him and said, "Who touched you, you're in the middle of this jostling pushing crowd, and you want to know who touched you?" And Jesus said, "I felt power go out of me."

And Sarah came forward. Poor woman, she has been ill—bleeding—for twelve years. She must have slipped into the crowd; she hasn't come out in crowds much during all this time. We did visit with her some, but only when the men were away, because a few of the men think she's unclean because of the bleeding and can pollute them before God. Now when the crowd saw it was Sarah, they drew back. But Jesus didn't, he didn't accuse her, as she knelt there trembling and telling her whole story. He called her daughter and said her trust had made her well. So Sarah again is one of us, out and about with us. We were delighted, though a few of the men seemed a bit uneasy with the way Jesus didn't care about those purity laws.

Then Jesus sent us out in pairs to preach and heal. Hannah and I went together. *We* went out and *we* proclaimed that the realm of God is here, and *we* healed, *we* cast out demons. God has given us too these powers to bring God's realm on earth.

Then there was this feeding of thousands. Jesus had been teaching this enormous group of people. And he turned and told us to feed them. And we said, "Feed them? Do you want us to go and spend thousands to buy food for all these people?" I admit, I couldn't believe what Jesus said. And Jesus said to feed them. "See what food you have." So we gathered what we could find and we found some loaves and a couple of fish.

Now Hannah and I, we've stretched food. We're pretty good at it; we've had to be. But nothing like this, nothing like this. We fed thousands, and we took up baskets of food left over. Jesus was right, gracious God provided us all with plenty to eat.

And then we got into the boat again. This time Jesus had sent us ahead and the men were rowing hard across the lake, and this figure came walking on the water. We were terrified, we thought it was a ghost! And it was Jesus, and he got into the boat with us. Who is this, who could walk on water?

A huge crowd gathered around Jesus again. Some scribes came down from Jerusalem to check Jesus out. They got debating with Jesus about the dietary laws, and he silenced them all, saying we could eat anything—that wasn't what was important. I love the way Jesus gets the best of these so-called authorities. But you know, with all these crowds following Jesus, it makes me a bit nervous too. Authorities don't like this.

And then Jesus took us to Gentile territory. This time we went to a village near Tyre and entered a house. Jesus was trying to keep himself hidden. He didn't want anyone to know he was there. Now I, Artemisia, I ask you who are listening to me, Do you really think he could do that? All those strangers arriving in a village? News travels fast in a village.

Now back to Ruth's story: Ruth says a pagan woman entered the house and came in the middle of them. She begged Jesus to heal her daughter, to cast the demon out of her little girl. And you know what Jesus said? He said, "Let the children first be fed because it is not right to take the children's bread and throw it to the dogs!"

Huh! Her child isn't even a child, she's just a dog, not worth feeding! I, Artemisia, I would have walked out then and there—this man wasn't going to act as patron for someone he called a dog. But according to Ruth, they weren't surprised at Jesus' way of talking. After all, in her eyes, the woman was an unclean Gentile, and Jesus and all of them were Jews, the people with God's laws–But the Syrophoenician woman didn't walk out, she turned to Jesus, politely called him "sir" as we were all taught to do, and told him, "Yeah, we may only be dogs, but look, sir, the little dogs under the table get the children's crumbs."

And Jesus—Jesus agreed with her. He said, "For your word, for what you have said, you may go your way. The demon has left your daughter." And when the woman got home, she found her daughter healed and the demon gone.

And again Jesus asked us to feed a huge crowd—Gentiles this time. The men with us murmured a bit. As for us women, maybe we were murmuring too. Anyway, we started gathering food. Jesus blessed it, and again a huge crowd was satisfied, and there was plenty left over.

And then we got into the boat again. I don't know which is worse, just being in the boat or what happens when we're in the boat. But at least this time nothing eerie happened. Instead we just got lectured. Jesus told us that *we* didn't understand, that *our* hearts were hardened. He asked, how many loaves did we feed the five thousand with, and we told him. And he asked how many baskets of food were left over, and we told him that. He asked how many loaves did we feed the four thousand with, and we told him, and how many baskets were left over, and we told him that. Now Hannah and I don't need a lesson in counting. We run a fish business. If we couldn't count, we would long since have lost our choice place in the market to Miriam and her daughter. They've been coveting our good place for years. But I don't understand what Jesus is trying to tell us; he just says our hearts are hardened.

Then we went on a journey way up north. At least this was a land journey and I didn't have to get into a boat. On the way, Jesus asked us, "Who do people say that I am?" And we told him, "Elijah, one of the prophets of old, John the Baptist." And then he said, "Who do *you* say that I am?" And Peter jumped in and said, "You are the Messiah!" Do you suppose maybe he is? I do know Jesus is someone special with God.

And Jesus went right on to say, "It is necessary for the Son of Humanity to endure many things, be rejected, killed, and on the third day rise." And Peter jumped right in again to correct Jesus. You never can get a word in ahead of Peter. You know, they say us women talk a lot, but we can't beat Peter. And Jesus turned to Peter, and called him Satan! But you know Peter had a point: why should Jesus who walks on water, who feeds thousands, and who can command demons; why should he be killed?

But Jesus didn't explain. Instead he told us it was to be our fate too. He called us and the whole crowd together and said, if we wanted to follow him, we had to turn away from our families, take up our crosses (that horrible and shameful means of execution the Romans use) and follow him. If we wanted to save our lives, we needed to lose them for his sake and the good news. But if we tried to save them, we would in fact lose them. I wish I understood Jesus better.

And again a little farther along—we were journeying south now—Jesus predicted he would be turned over to authorities, and they would kill him, and on the third day he would rise. The men with us, they were debating among themselves, which one of *them* was the greatest among us. Really! And Jesus knew what they were saying and rebuked them and told us all, "Whoever wants to be first among you must be least of all and servant of all." And to show what he meant, he picked up a child. As you know, these days, the child is one of the weakest, one with the least power, the most downtrodden—I'm glad I'm not a child anymore. So Jesus picked up a child, a little girl about two. He picked her up and blessed her, and he said if we wanted to enter God's realm, we needed to be least like she was least.

And then as we were traveling along, a young man came to us—you could tell he was wealthy, not one of us, by his clothes. And he asked Jesus, what he had to do to inherit eternal life. And after they talked a while, Jesus told him, "Go sell what you have, give to the poor, and come follow me." And he went away sad, he couldn't do that.

And again Peter, Peter asked the question: Peter said, "We've left everything and followed you." I'm glad Peter asked that. I'm not sure I would have dared after the rebuke Peter got, getting called Satan. And Jesus said, "Whoever has left houses and fathers and mothers and brothers and sisters and lands and fields for my sake and for the good news, will gain again in this age mothers, sisters and brothers, fields and houses—with persecutions—and in the age to come, eternal life.

You know he's right. We are like a family. I like this new community of which we are a part. And you notice what he didn't say–he didn't say there was a new father. We didn't get a new person to order us around, whom we women are taught, it is always our duty to obey. We are indeed a group together, all with Jesus.

We were approaching Jerusalem now, with this enormous crowd of people ahead and following. And a third time, Jesus predicted that he was going to endure many things, be rejected, crucified, and on the third day rise. By now, I'm afraid he really will be crucified. You couldn't expect to go into Jerusalem with a crowd like this and not get into trouble—unless of course God's about to bring about the end of the age. You know, I've heard about all the troubles and woes, the labor pains bringing in the new age, but I don't know that I like it.

And James and John are at it again. After Jesus predicted his execution and his rising, they went and asked him if they could have the seats of glory and power on his right and left in the age to come! And Jesus asked them, could they endure what he would endure, could they drink the cup he would drink, undergo the baptism he was going to undergo? I don't know if I could, but then I've born five children, and I know what labor pains are like. James and John said they could. But they didn't get those seats—Jesus didn't give them any reward. He said to them, "Okay! If you are able to endure persecution, you will, but don't think it's any heroic suffering that'll get you a special reward in the new age."

And we went on into Jerusalem, and Jesus caused a big to-do in the temple. I thought Jesus would be arrested then and there, but he wasn't. We got out safely and the next days he continued teaching everyone, besting all the authorities who tried to trap him in his speech.

And pretty soon, Jesus instructed us to prepare the Passover meal, and we all ate with him, and it was really very, very sad. He told us this was his last meal with us—he would not drink wine again until he drank it anew in the realm of God.

After dinner, we went out to the Mount of Olives. Jesus was praying, and he asked us to keep watch. But we were dozing and sleeping–it had been a big meal. Suddenly soldiers came and arrested Jesus. The men, the male disciples we've been traveling with, they all took off, they just fled, leaving us alone in the middle of the night with a bunch of soldiers. And there we were, Hannah and me and the other women. Now Hannah said, "The men are in more danger. The soldiers were more likely to arrest them than us." But I said to her, "Yes, but remember, they do crucify women too. Besides, you know what soldiers do to women out alone at night. That's not a very good idea either." But we did get back safely to where we were staying. They must have been too busy dealing with Jesus.

The Romans crucified him the next day. We went out and watched Jesus die on the cross. Hannah and I and the other women, we went and watched. We stood a ways off. I could hardly see through my tears. I think Jesus saw us, I think he knew we were there watching. I think he was comforted.

And then after he cried out and died, we went and watched where they buried him. And the next morning very early we went out to the tomb to prepare his body properly for burial, which we hadn't been able to do. And there was a young person at the tomb, someone in dazzling white, maybe an angel, he or maybe she, I don't know. The angel told us not to be afraid, Jesus had gone before us to Galilee, and to go tell Peter and the other men to go to Galilee, to the place where the realm of God began. There we will see him. We were terrified, we were awestruck. Just like the men earlier, we now fled, we ran away. We ran as fast as we could away from there, away. We were utterly overwhelmed. We didn't tell anyone anything. We were afraid.

Ruth said. "Every one of you who has ears to hear, listen for this is the good news of Jesus Christ." And as the daylight faded, Artemisia said to those gathered around her in the village square. "Here ends the Gospel of Ruth."

Notes on Performing

This script is not meant to be read silently to oneself, as we read today. Nor is it meant to be read aloud to a group. It is meant to be performed orally with lots of emotion and expression. I have not memorized the script; I am thoroughly familiar with it and I compose it anew every time in the process of telling it as ancient oral performers customarily did. There are always variations in my telling. I use a "cheat sheet," a small two-by-six card, on which I have listed the various scenes in order. Thus, in telling, I can concentrate on the scene I am narrating, imagining it in my mind, and then glance at the sheet to check what comes next.

I encourage you to make the script your own and to tell it. Feel free to elaborate it, to ham it up, to modify it. I change my voice, I speed up the tempo, and I slow it way down towards the end. Tell it as it feels right to you, and pass it on.

Questions

1. Identify a story that you often tell that has been passed on to you by someone else. In what ways is your telling of the story different than the telling of the one who first told it to you?

2. What does the author of this chapter mean by "androcentric"? In what ways is Mark's gospel androcentric? In what ways are we as readers or hearers of that gospel androcentric?

3. What difference do you think it makes to hear this story told from the perspective of a woman?

4

ORAL PERFORMANCE IN THE NEW TESTAMENT WORLD

WHITNEY SHINER

PERFORMANCE CRITICISM OF NEW TESTAMENT TEXTS IS based on the historical observation that the texts were originally intended for oral performance.[1] It is estimated that in the first century only ten percent of the people in the Roman Empire could read.[2] That estimate includes many people who could only sound out words with some difficulty or could read only well enough to get by if their job required them to maintain an inventory, for example, or perform some other task that required minimal literacy. It is very unlikely that very many of that ten per cent could read a book with any fluency for the simple reason that books were very expensive, and only the very rich could afford to own any.

There was another more important reason, however, for the performance of texts. In the first century, writing was largely understood as a representation of speech. Oral communication was understood as true communication. A book was a list of words waiting to become communication. Even when a person read to herself, she usually read aloud to re-create the sound of the words. We find fairly often in the ancient

---

1. Much of the material in this chapter is adapted from Whitney Shiner, *Proclaiming the Gospel: First-Century Performance of Mark* (Harrisburg, PA: Trinity, 2003). Another evaluation of oral performance in the New Testament world that shares many of the same conclusions can be found in William Shiell, *Reading Acts: The Lector and the Early Christian Audience* (Boston: Brill Academic, 2004).

2. William V. Harris, *Ancient Literacy* (Cambridge: Harvard University Press, 1989) 22, 272, 259.

world a contrast between the living word of oral communication and the dead word of a written text. One well known example of this attitude is found in the words of Papias, a Christian who wrote in the first half of the second century C.E.. Papias says he had spoken to the followers of the disciples of Jesus whenever he had a chance because, "I did not suppose that information from books would help me so much as the word of a living and surviving voice."[3] There are a number of reasons oral communication was regarded as the living voice. Communication was understood as taking place between actual people involved in a relationship of one kind or another. The physical presence of the speaker is an important part of the communication. Oral communication adapts like a living organism. The Greek philosopher Plato argued that writing provides only the semblance of wisdom instead of true teaching. If you question a book, he pointed out, the written word cannot respond but dumbly repeats the same thing. A book does not know how to judge its audience to know when to speak and when to remain silent.[4]

An eloquent comparison between spoken and written speech is found in the writing of Isocrates, an Athenian of the fourth century B.C.E. and the first "orator" who composed written speeches which he did not deliver himself. He was clearly aware of the disadvantage at which he was placed by not performing the speeches himself, and makes this plea in a written "oration" that he sent to be read to Philip of Macedonia, the father of Alexander the Great.

> And yet I do not fail to realize what a great difference there is in persuasiveness between discourses which are spoken and those which are to be read . . . for when a discourse is robbed of the prestige of the speaker, the tones of his voice, the variations which are made in the delivery, . . . and when someone reads it aloud without persuasiveness and without putting any personal feeling into it, but as though he were repeating a table of figures,—in these circumstances it is natural, I think, that it should make an indifferent impression upon its hearers.[5]

The living voice is, however, a fleeting voice. Since no oral performances of the Gospels or the other writings of the New Testament remain,

---

3. Quoted by Eusebius *Ecclesiastical History* 3.39.1–4 (Lake, LCL).

4. Plato *Phaedrus* 275a-e

5. Isocrates *Orations* 5.25–27 (Norlin, LCL).

what can we know about the way they were performed? While the details of any one performance can never be recovered, we can understand the cultural ideal of performance which would be expected by audiences and which performers would strive to emulate. We can know that by looking at descriptions of performances from the first century and reading instructions about how to speak effectively. One of our important sources for understanding speaking style in the first century is a man named Quintilian, who ran a famous school of public speaking in Rome and wrote a book with detailed instructions, probably for his own students.

The Performance Ideal

The ability to speak well was highly prized in the ancient Mediterranean world. It was one of the principle means of social advancement. Speaking well was valued by many in early Christian communities as well, as shown by the charge made by the opponents of Paul that "his bodily presence is weak, and his speech of no account" (2 Cor 10:10). Good speakers were admired and attracted the sorts of large crowds that we would associate with rock stars. Crowds would fill up theaters to hear a famous rhetorician from out of town. Large crowds would gather to listen to the speeches given in the law courts even when the case being argued was not of particular interest.

There would be a range of performance styles depending on the situation of the performance. Relating a short version of a story in an informal setting would probably be done in a more subdued style than a longer narration or an argument presented in a more formal setting (on informal storytelling see chapter 2). Clearly the crowds loved flamboyant speaking styles and frequently applauded as much for a speaker's style as for substance.

Reading and Reciting from Memory

It is certainly possible that some, if not all of the gospels, were orally composed, and that our texts are simply one version of a fluid oral narrative. Studies of oral narrative show that works of that length do not have a fixed word-for-word text. Instead, a significant part of the narrative is spontaneously composed again for each performance. The same possibility exists for some other New Testament works such as Revelation or the letter of James. Other works, such as the letters of Paul, were composed as written works. Paul would have composed them as he went along, speaking to a scribe who wrote down his composition. At some point, though, many works that existed first as oral compositions were written down. How would these texts be presented?

Most written works in the first century were placed on scrolls. A form of book similar to that of modern books did exist (the form known as a *codex*), but it was generally used for inventories and other mundane tasks. Anything important was put on a scroll. Sometimes statues of orators or playwrights include scrolls grasped in one hand. The scroll is included as a badge of their professions, but it is very rare that they are shown reading from the scroll. Scrolls were extremely cumbersome to read. Generally someone reading from a scroll sat at a table on which the scroll was placed. The reader had to use both hands to roll through the scroll whenever she moved from one column to another. At least in Greek, all the words were run together into a continuous line of letters. For the most part there was no punctuation to help the reader make out the sense of the text. So even if one was reading directly from the scroll, almost all readers would have to spend a considerable amount of time working through the meaning of the text before it was read in public.

Reading, acting, and rhetorical delivery were considered related skills, and the same word could be used for all three. Pliny the Younger, an aristocrat who had a very successful political career, employed an actor who performed for dinner parties as both a reader and an actor.[6] Quintilian invited famous actors to his school as models from whom his students could learn effective voice inflection and gestures for their speeches.[7] He warns against the exaggerated gestures used by actors of comedy, but the distinction appears to be one of degree, and a fairly small degree at that. A large part of his concern with speaking in exactly the same style as the actors is an issue of class and prestige. Actors were very popular, but they were considered to be dissolute, and acting was not a respectable profession for the upper-class young men who came to his school.

Because extemporaneous speech was valued as a cultural ideal, written material would be memorized if it was considered important and if

---

6. Pliny *Letters* 5.19.
7. Quintilian 1.11.12 (Butler, LCL).

the length of the writing allowed. As soon as they learned to read, students were expected to memorize written material for recitation. Rhetoricians typically memorized speeches even if they lasted several hours or more. Quintilian warns his students not to read their speeches, because judges in law courts would consider it disrespectful.[8] All New Testament writings are short enough to have been memorized for performance, and because of the expectations of the culture, they probably would have been.

It would not be considered necessary to memorize a written text verbatim. This would be particularly true with gospel material that existed in oral tradition as well as in written form. The variations among parallel sayings and stories found in the Synoptic Gospels probably reflect the type of variations found in memorized performances. It was generally, though not universally, thought that Matthew knew a written version of Mark. If that is correct, Matthew feels perfectly free to add and leave out material, to change the order of stories, and to change many details. A look at any synopsis of the Gospels, that prints parallel stories in parallel columns, shows constant variation between stories. For example, Mark's story of the exorcism of demons into a herd of swine extends for twenty verses (Mark 5:1–20), while in Matthew's version of the story (Matt 8:26–39) contains fewer details and is considerably shorter. Students in more or less the equivalent of American middle school learned to expand and condense stories in this way.[9] The two versions of the story also differ concerning the number of demoniacs (one or two) as well as the location of the event (country of the Gerasenes or of the Gadarenes), and the types of details that storytellers (though not modern historians) would feel free to fill in themselves. It is highly likely that both Mark's and Matthew's versions would be considered faithful reproductions of the story. It is highly unlikely that a performer of a written text, who did not have the text in front of her, would have been any more concerned with reproducing the text exactly than writers like Matthew or Luke, who might have been able to consult a text if they cared to.

One might think that the exact form of the stories might have been considered sacrosanct, on the model of Jewish Scripture. This is unlikely to have been the case in the first century, but even if it had been, Scripture

---

8. Quintilian 11.3.132.

9. Burton L. Mack, "Elaboration of the Chreia in the Hellenistic School," in Burton L. Mack and Vernon K. Robbins, *Patterns of Persuasion in the Gospels* (Sonoma, CA: Polebridge, 1989) 31–67.

does not appear to have been considered a verbatim fixed text. Greek and Aramaic versions of biblical texts contain considerable material not found in the modern canonical text. For example, the Greek version of Daniel contains in chapter 14 accounts of Daniel destroying a statue of the Babylonian god Bel and slaying a dragon worshiped by the Babylonians (Septuagint Dan 14:1–30), neither of which is found in the modern canonical version. The same comparative freedom is shown in the variations in wording found when Scripture is quoted. In a number of places New Testament writers combine different passages of Scripture into one "quote." For example, the quotation from Isaiah with which Mark begins his Gospel (1:2–3) is a composite of either Exod 23:20 or Mal 3:1 (v. 2b), or Isa 40:3, with free composition holding the two parts together (Mark 1:2c).

The ideal of extemporaneous speech would allow for considerable addition or subtraction of material in order to address a particular audience or situation. Flexibility in the performance of individual episodes of the gospels would also be consistent with cultural norms. Quintilian urged his more advanced students to be free in departing from the written version of their speech they had used to commit the speech to memory. He felt that our words should flow from the subject on which we are speaking rather than our memory. Preparation and memory are tools for allowing us to speak better. The crowning achievement in the study of rhetoric, he says, is the ability to improvise.[10]

Narrative Style

One of the most important rules of narration was to make the events vividly present to the audience. The great Roman orator and statesman Cicero says, "great effect may be produced . . . by setting forth our facts in such a striking manner that they seem to be placed before the eyes as vividly as if they were taking place in our actual presence."[11] Hans Dieter Betz has, I think correctly, suggested that Paul's statement in Gal 3:1, "It

---

10. Quintilian 10.6.5–7.

11. Cicero *On the Making of an Orator* 3.53.202 (quoted in Quintilian, 9.1.27 [Butler, LCL]).

was before your eyes that Jesus Christ was publicly exhibited as crucified," refers to such a vivid narration of the passion of Jesus.[12]

One of the rhetorical textbooks gives a description of the way narrative should be presented in a speech, and it seems very likely that anyone presenting a story such as a gospel would use the same method.

> Varied intonations are necessary, so that we seem to recount everything just as it took place. Our delivery will be somewhat rapid when we narrate what we wish to show was done vigorously, and it will be slower when we narrate something else done in leisurely fashion. Then, corresponding to the content of the words, we shall modify the delivery in all the kinds of tone, now to sharpness, now to kindness, or now to sadness, and now to gaiety . . . we shall give careful attention to expressing with the voice the feelings and thoughts of each personage.[13]

Clearly the author is describing the sort of storytelling technique that we would expect today. Dialog would have been presented in character with emotions of the character reflected in the performance. At least limited voice differentiation of characters might be employed. Our friend Quintilian, also describing the use of narrative within speech, says the tone of voice should fit the character of the person impersonated and reflect the feeling of that person.[14] Quintilian felt that the orator should not go to the extremes of mimicry found on the comic stage, but it is clear from his complaints that in the popular style of oratory, the distinction between oratory and acting was often lost.[15]

Ancient characters tended to fall into types. On the stage the character type was represented by a limited number of masks that helped the audience anticipate the nature of the character's speech and action. Performance of narrative would not involve masks, but the audience would tend to categorize characters into conventional types. Someone performing a gospel would probably indicate to the audience through their tone and gesture which of the character types was appropriate for each person in the narrative.

12. Hans Dieter Betz, *Galatians*, Hermeneia (Philadelphia: Fortress: 1979) 131.

13. *Rhetorica ad Herennium* 3.14.24 (Caplan, LCL).

14. Quintilian 11.1.39–42.

15. Quintilian 11.3.182–84.

Voice and Gesture

To some extent, the type of performance style was the result of the situation in which most performances were given. Generally, speeches and other forms of oral performance were presented outdoors before large and often rowdy crowds. While some outdoor theaters had very good acoustics, many speeches were given in large open squares. A loud booming voice was a necessity if the speaker was going to be heard. While the closer members of the audience could see a speaker's facial expressions, those on the outskirts of the crowd could only see large dramatic gestures. In the theater, actors faces were covered by masked that served to identify roles and personality types. Because the face was covered, emotion could only be expressed by bodily gestures. As a result actors and audiences developed a standardized set of body and hand gestures to express various emotions.[16] It is clear from the textbooks on public speaking that orators made use of many of the same gestures. Sometimes such gestures are indicated in narrative, such as in Mark 3:5, where it is said that Jesus "looked around at them with anger." In other places the gesture seems to be assumed, as in Mark 3:34: "Here are my mother and my brothers!" which suggests a gesture including the audience as the mother and brothers. In oratory, gesturing was nearly constant. Quintilian warns his students against using too many gestures, but when he gives an example of how to match gestures with stresses within a sentence, he indicates eight movements for a single seventeen word sentence.[17] This was probably the case for narrative delivery as well.

Ancient delivery was extremely bombastic when judged by contemporary western standards. Quintilian suggests that many people, especially among the lower classes, preferred extreme vigor in rhetorical delivery. He characterizes the approach of such orators as follows:

> They shout on all and every occasion and bellow their every utterance "with uplifted hand," to use their own phrase, dashing this

16. A large number of theatrical gestures are found in illustrations included in some copies of the plays of Terence. The original illustrations date from the third century CE. L. W. Jones and C. R. Morey, *The Miniatures of the Manuscripts of Terence prior to the 13th Century*, 2 vols. (Princeton: Princeton University Press, 1930–1931). An extensive selection of the Terrence miniatures is included in C. R. Dodwell, *Anglo-Saxon Gestures and the Roman Stage*, Cambridge Studies in Anglo-Saxon England 28 (Cambridge: Cambridge University Press, 2000).

17. Quintilian 11.3.106–110.

way and that, panting, gesticulating wildly and wagging their heads with all the frenzy of a lunatic. Smite your hands together, stamp the ground, slap your thigh, your breast, your forehead, and you will go straight to the heart of the dingier members of your audience.[18]

He criticizes orators who address their subjects in a wild and exclamatory manner, beginning with a shriek and keeping their presentation at one high level of violence.[19] He takes to task those who "feel that they have fallen short of eloquence, if they do not make everything echo with noise and clamour"[20] and who make use of "affected modulations of the voice, throwing back their heads, thumping their sides and indulging in every kind of extravagance of statement, language and style."[21] Other orators appear too much like actors, with affected delivery, annoyingly restless gestures, and too frequent changes in vocal tone.[22]

Emotion

The important role of emotion in creating meaning for both narrative and argumentative works has until recently been largely ignored by scholars seeking to unlock the meaning of biblical texts. From the time of classical Greek culture, the importance of emotion was stressed both by literary theorists and by writers who describe contemporary practice. Emotion was so important in drama that the philosopher Aristotle defined tragedy in terms of emotion: Emotional release or catharsis, he states, is the very purpose of tragic drama.[23]

A performer's ability was largely judged on the depth of emotion the performance elicited from the audience. The Greeks and later the Romans included contests between rhapsodes, men who performed the epics of Homer, in games such as the Olympics which were dedicated to the gods. Ion, a rhapsode who appears in one of Plato's writings, says that he knows

---

18. Quintilian 2.12.9–10 (Butler, LCL); cf. Quintilian's summary of popular style in 12.10.73.

19. Quintilian 3.8.59–60.

20. Quintilian 4.2.37 (Butler, LCL).

21. Quintilian 4.2.39 (Butler, LCL).

22. Quintilian 11.3.183.

23. On the central role of emotionalism in Greek performance art, see W. B. Stanford, *Greek Tragedy and the Emotions: An Introductory Study* (London: Routledge & Kegan Paul, 1983) 1–10.

he will not receive the prize in a competition if he does not see his audience weeping, casting terrible glances, and stricken with amazement.[24]

The writers on rhetoric also stress the importance of emotions and recognized that emotion was superior to rational argument in convincing an audience.[25] Our friend Quintilian says, "it is in its power over the emotions that the life and soul of oratory is to be found."[26] While a lawyer should be able to make sound arguments,

> the peculiar task of the orator arises when the minds of the judges
> . . . have actually to be led away from the contemplation of the
> truth . . . Proofs, it is true, may induce the judges to regard our case
> as superior to that of our opponent, but the appeal to the emotions
> will do more, for it will make them wish our case to be the better
> . . . so the judge, when overcome by his emotions, abandons all
> attempt to enquire into the truth of the arguments, is swept along
> by the tide of passion, and yields himself unquestioning to the rent
> . . . when the judge has been really moved by the orator he reveals
> his feelings while he is still sitting and listening to the case. When
> those tears, which are the aim of most perorations, well forth from
> his eyes, is he not giving his verdict for all to see?[27]

Among the important emotions an orator would seek to stir in his audience are good will toward oneself and one's cause and ill will toward one's opponents. So, for example, the opponents of Jesus in the gospels are often depicted as devious or attacked as hypocrites or lovers of money (Mark 7:6–12; Matt 23:13–36; Luke 16:14).

To give one example from the gospels, the effectiveness of Mark's crucifixion scene (Mark 15:16–39) results in no small part from the interplay of the two emotions felt by the audience. The suffering of Jesus evokes pity. The arrogance of the mockers evokes anger. The rapid interplay between the suffering of Jesus and the ignorance of those mocking creates a surreal scene that brings to a climax the split between the apparent

24. Plato *Ion* 535e.

25. Thomas H. Olbricht, "Pathos As Proof in Greco-Roman Rhetoric," in *Paul and Pathos*, ed. Thomas H. Olbricht and Jerry L. Sumney, 7–22 SBL Symposium Series 16 (Atlanta: Society of Biblical Literature, 2001); Carol Poster, "The Affections of the Soul: Pathos, Protreptic, and Preaching in Hellenistic Thought," in *Paul and Pathos,* 23–37; Steven J. Kirkchick, "Pathos in Paul: The Emotional Logic of 'Original Argument,'" in *Paul and Pathos*, 39–68.

26. Quintilian 6.2.7.

27. Quintilian 6.2.4–7 (Butler, LCL).

(the judgment of people) and the real (the judgment of God) that is emphasized throughout the Gospel.[28]

A number of writers emphasized the importance of the speaker actually participating in the emotions that she sought to elicit in her audience. For example, Pliny says,

> The orator ought in fact to be roused and heated, sometimes even to boiling-point, and to let his feelings carry him on till he treads the edge of a precipice; for a path along the heights and peaks often skirts the sheer drop below. It may be safer to keep to the plain, but the road lies too low to be interesting.[29]

It is clear that the meaning of a performance is found at least as much in the emotions produced as in any propositions stated. This is one of the things that sets performance criticism at odds with much other scholarly interpretation, since traditionally interpretation has focused on deriving intellectual meaning from texts. Performance criticism is much more open ended, since it draws the audience into a lived encounter with the situations portrayed by the text. The full encounter between the person and the situation made alive from out of the text is more conducive to spiritual formation than to the development of doctrine. For example, the passion of Jesus is sometimes reduced to something like "Jesus died for your sins," while the story of the crucifixion in Mark never suggests such a doctrinal interest. Instead, the audience is led through a series of rejections of Jesus by those with power, such as the crowds of people in Jerusalem (Mark 15:6–15), the Roman soldiers (Mark 15:16–20, 23–24), passers-by who are allowed by the Romans to participate in the spectacle of the execution (Mark 15:29–30, 35–36), and chief priests and scribes (Mark 15:31–32). Anyone paying any attention in the audience experiences a similar series of rejections by those who could have made the message of Jesus the policy of Roman Judea and the consequent need to choose between the word of Jesus and the word of human power and authority. To take another example, in Mark 3:35, Jesus states, "Whoever does the will of God is my brother and sister and mother," which might suggest intellectually some standard for being accepted by Jesus (if we could figure out what qualifies as "the will of God"), but for the audience

---

28. On this issue, see especially Joel Marcus, "Mark 4:10–12 and Marcan Epistemology," *Journal of Biblical Literature* 103 (1984) 557–74.

29. Pliny *Letters* 9.26.1 (Radice, LCL).

it is more likely to be experienced as an invitation, along the lines of, "Do the will of God (as best you can understand it), and Jesus accepts you as a brother, a sister, or his mother."

Audience

Audiences were actively involved in oral performances. They cheered for well-turned phrases as well as for opinions they shared. They jeered mercilessly at poor performances and persons and opinions they disapproved. Our aristocratic friend Pliny expresses shock when two men who came to a friend's recitation sit quietly throughout, never opening their lips, stirring their hands, or rising to their feet. He considers such behavior to be absolutely boorish and insulting.[30] Various forms of applause indicated various levels of approval. Raising the hand was a mild form of applause.[31] Standing indicated a more emphatic applause.[32] Even more enthusiasm was shown by rushing forward toward the speaker.[33] Horace describes leaping up and thumping the ground with one's foot as forms of applause.[34] Clapping was a common form of applause in the theater.[35] The most common form of applause was for the audience to yell out expressions of approval. Greek audiences yelled approbations such as beautiful!, wise!, and true!, stinging!, clever!, and flowery!, as well as more extravagant praises such as divine!, inspired by a god!, and unapproachable![36] Audience reaction was such an important part of a performance that speakers or artists often hired people to applaud at the proper time. These sorts of applause lines are frequently found in the gospels after healing. "They were all amazed and glorified God, saying, 'We have never seen anything like this!'" (Mark 2:12). When Jesus teaches in Capernaum, "they were all astounded at his teaching" (Mark 1:22) probably indicates verbal expressions of praise, and the hubbub in the crowd after the

---

30. Pliny *Letters* 6.17.1–3.

31. Lucian *Essays in Portaiture Defended* 4.

32. Lucian 4; *A Professor of Public Speaking* 22; Plutarch, *On Listening to Lectures* 41c; Quintilian 2.2.9.

33. Quintilian 2.2.9.

34. Horace *Art of Poetry* 430.

35. Horace *Letters* 2.1.205.

36. Quintilian 2.2.9; Plutarch *On Listening to Lectures* 41c, 44d, 45f–46a.

exorcism (Mark 1:27) appears to be partly question, partly shouted praise, "'What is this?' 'A new teaching!' 'With authority!' 'He commands even the unclean spirits!' And they obey him.'" Audiences were equally outspoken in their disapproval. A number of interactions between speakers and hecklers have been recorded. Sometimes the speaker gets the better of the exchange, sometimes the heckler. We find an audience heckling Jesus in Mark's story of Jesus' trip to his hometown, where his teaching in the synagogue is drowned out by derision from the audience. "'Where did this man get all this?' 'What deeds of power are being done by his hands!' 'Is this not the carpenter?' 'The son of Mary!' 'And brother of James and Joses!' 'And Judas and Simon!' 'And aren't his sisters here with us?'" (Mark 6:2–3). While Jesus usually puts those who question him in their place, his response here is rather tepid: "Prophets are not without honor, except in their hometown, and among their own kin, and in their own house" (Mark 6:4). That makes a point with Mark's audience, but clearly does not win over the hometown folk. In other cases, Jesus' audience is even more emphatic in their disapproval, deciding to throw stones at him (John 8:59; 10:31) or throw him off a cliff (Luke 4:29).

Roman audiences looked for associations between narrative and their own situation. For example, Cicero reports that in 59 B.C.E., theater audiences wildly applauded lines such as, "By our misfortunes are you great," and, "In time to come you will lament your boldness," which they interpreted references to the triumvir Pompey, who had fallen out of favor with the crowd. The first line the actor "was forced to speak a thousand times."[37] That should alert us to the possibility that audiences may be reading symbolic meanings into a performance that are not obvious on the surface. One might expect, for example, that various passages referring to bread would be heard by early Christians in the context of the eucharist (multiplication of loaves, Mark 6:30–44; 8:1–9, and parallel passages in other gospels; the discussion about bread in John 6:25–59; the one loaf in Mark 8:14). The naming of the demons as "Legion," a reference to the Roman army, seems like an open invitation to read the destruction of the demons that follows as a destruction of the occupying forces.

We see something similar operating in the way that Christians reuse material from Jewish Scripture, seeing in it references to Jesus and their

---

37. Cicero *Letters to Atticus* 2.19. For political use of crowd acclamations in Rome, principally in regard to emperors, see Gregory S. Aldrete, *Gestures and Acclamations in Ancient Rome* (Baltimore: Johns Hopkins University Press, 1999) 101–71.

present situation. So the passage from Jeremiah, referring to a situation in the time of Jeremiah, becomes in Matthew (2:18) a reference to things that happened during the early childhood of Jesus. A passage from Joel appears in Acts (1:17–21) to refer to the present situation of the apostles speaking in tongues (though parts of the passage, such as the sun turning to darkness and the moon to blood do not seem to have any current reference). A passage in Deuteronomy referring to the law is used by Paul to refer to faith in Jesus (Rom 10:6–8).

Conclusions

It is clear from the stress placed on the importance of delivery, or the proper performance of written and oral works in the first century C.E., that we can only understand the works of the New Testament in their historical context through the oral performance of those works. There are some aspects of the texts that can only be understood in performance, such as the emotional tone of the texts. There are other aspects of the Bible that can only be understood by thinking about the performance of the texts in their original situation. If the oral performance of a text had more to do with the authority of the performer than the authority of a text that had not yet acquired the sort of verbatim authority we associate with Scriptural authority, how are we to understand the authority of a particular version of a fluid oral text which happened to be written down and handed on to the later church? If a text can be performed in a variety of ways, how can we determine which performance is "the Word of God"? Thinking about the way that New Testament texts were experienced in the early church does not give us easy answers to these questions. Instead, we find an authority that is based partly on the personal spiritual authority of the speaker, partly on the way that the speaker embodies the tradition of Jesus, and partly on the way that the audience, the church, accepts or rejects the interpretation of the tradition about Jesus.

Questions

1. What qualities would an audience in the ancient world expect an effective speaker to demonstrate?

2. Identify a context today in which you encounter someone "performing" a text. What qualities would an audience today expect an effective speaker to demonstrate? How does the context in which the speech-act takes place shape these expectations? How does the make-up of the audience shape these expectations?

3. Memorize a short text for performance. First imagine yourself as a speaker in the ancient world. Consider what gestures you will employ, what tone of voice, what pace you will employ in recitation in order to effectively communicate with your audience. Now transport yourself to the modern world. How will you need to alter your performance in order to communicate effectively?

5

COMPETING GOSPELS

Imperial Echoes, A Dissident Voice

Arthur J. Dewey

Indeed, I'm not ashamed of the good news, because it is God's effec-tive way to deliver everyone who has trust, the Jew first, and also the Greek. (Rom 1:16, Scholars Version)

IT IS ALTOGETHER FITTING IN THIS CELEBRATION OF THE work of Tom Boomershine to take up the question of Pauline dissonance. Just as Tom has often presented a dissenting voice within the world of biblical studies, so too Paul represented a dissenting voice within the im-perial world. In the first century C.E. Rome provided the good news for the world. This was the "gospel" people were accustomed to hearing and upon which they relied. Paul, nevertheless, went against the cultural and political grain by presenting a competing report to communities of Jesus followers in Rome.

In this essay I investigate the "surround sound" in which Paul deliv-ered his words to these Roman communities by describing the acoustical default setting for those living within the Roman Empire. Within that setting the letter to the Romans takes on a tone of significant dissonance. We shall see that Rom 1:1–7 becomes a remarkable affront to the powers that be; that Rom 10:4–13 reiterates this audacity as it indicates how the voices of those unheard of come to speech; and that remarks in Rom 12 and 13 not only show the shrewd wisdom of one living in an empire but also echo and further the theopolitical thrust of the entire letter.

The Acoustical Default of the Empire

To detect the "surround sound system" in which the Letter to the Romans was originally heard, one can only proceed by an indirect path. Let us venture down this path by considering how the term "gospel" (*euangelion*) was heard within the imperial atmosphere of the Roman Empire.

It is often assumed that the term "gospel" (*euangelion*) occurs only within the context of the New Testament. Of course, many scholars have made a distinction between the use of this word by Paul and the writers of the Gospels, but this still limits "gospel" to its use within the canon. By confining the word to this context investigators remain insensible to how it was heard within the probable echo chamber of the ancient world.

In fact, the term was already part and parcel of the Roman propaganda machine that helped establish and maintain the Augustan revolution. A decree issued by the Provincial Assembly of Asia, in 9 B.C.E. is illustrative. This decree, recorded in the Priene Inscription, presents the benefits of Roman peace as the reason for the worship of the emperor. Here we encounter the default way of understanding *euangelion*.

> Whereas the Providence [*Pronoia*] which has regulated our whole existence, and which has shown such care and liberality, has brought our life to the climax of perfection in giving to us Augustus, whom it filled with virtue for the welfare of men, and who, being sent to us and our descendents as a Savior [*sōtēr*], has put an end to war and has set all things in order; and having become manifest [*phaneis*], Caesar has fulfilled all the hopes of earlier times . . . , not only in surpassing all the benefactors [*euergetai*] who preceded him but also in leaving to his successors no hope of surpassing him; and whereas, finally the birthday of the god has been for the whole world the beginning of good news [*euangelion*] concerning him [therefore, let a new era begin with his birth, and let his birthday mark the beginning of the new year].[1]

Helmut Koester argued that this usage of the term *euangelion* was new in the Greco-Roman world, in that "it elevates this term and equips it with a particular dignity." He then adds that "most likely . . . early Christian missionaries were influenced by the imperial propaganda in their employment of the word."[2] Koester moved quickly on to his primary concern, the

---

1. Frederick C. Grant, ed., *Ancient Roman Religion* (Indianapolis: Liberal Arts, 1957) 174.

2. Helmut Koester, *Ancient Christian Gospels* (Philadelphia: Trinity, 1990) 4.

early Christian collections of sayings and narrative material; however, it is crucial for this investigation not to leave the scene of the evidence too soon. The term *euangelion* cannot be read in isolation from its Roman imperial context.

The Priene Inscription was part of a complex propaganda project. The language in the inscription not only reinforced the accomplishments of the emperor Augustus (63 B.C.E.—14 C.E.) but placed him in the mythic realm of Alexander the Great. Like Alexander, Augustus was seen as having been sent to deliver the world from barbarism and disunity and bring about the order and harmony of a civilized world.[3] Virgil describes this new order as a golden age now underway.[4] Thus, the use of the term *euangelion* in the Priene Inscription evoked a larger cultural complex of action and imagination, song and ritual in calling forth devotion to the emperor. In doing so it sustained a particular vision of the world.

Further examples of Roman propaganda can be found among imperial artifacts. The Myra inscription, for instance, found at Myra in Lycia and dated to the early first century C.E., reiterated what was proclaimed at Priene:

> The god Augustus, Son of God, Caesar, Autocrat of land and sea,
> the Benefactor and Savior of the whole cosmos, the people of Myra
> [have set up this statue].[5]

In the Ara Pacis (Altar of Peace), commissioned by the Roman senate in 13 B.C.E. and consecrated in 9 B.C.E., we see another example of the imperial propaganda system. The altar celebrates Augustus' conquest and pacification of regions in Spain and Gaul. Marble screens around the altar portray a dedicatory scene in which the piety of Augustus is demonstrated. Engaged in a sacrificial procession, Augustus recapitulates the figure of the legendary Aeneas, who was regarded as the primordial ancestor of Rome and the embodiment of genuine virtue and fidelity. Augustus, veiled in the act of sacrifice, takes over the pious characteristics of Aeneas. This extensive configuring of *pietas* (devotion, fidelity, loyalty) reinforced what Virgil had already published in the new propaganda confabulation for Roman youth: the *Aeneid*. What was heard in the *Aeneid* about the virtue of Aeneas now comes to life in stone.

---

3. Cf. Plutarch *De Alex. Fort.* 1.8.

4. See *Aeneid* book 6; also his pastoral poem in the Fourth Ecologue.

5. Grant, *Ancient Roman Religion*, 175.

The *Gemma Augustea*, a small onyx cameo produced between 10 and 20 C.E., succinctly illustrates the "gospel" of the imperial world. In this cameo Augustus sits enthroned as Son of God, with Jupiter's eagle at his feet and Jupiter's spear in his left hand. He is being crowned by the goddess of peace, Irene, while captives of the Alpine and Danube areas await their deadly fate below. As the Roman soldiers in the lower left erect a trophy, the message is clear: order is maintained by violent control. On the upper left, dressed in a triumphal robe, Tiberius descends from his chariot. Behind him is the figure of Victory, and the young man in military dress between him and Roma, the goddess of Rome, is his nephew, Germanicus, son of his brother, Drusus. Nevertheless, the triumphs belong to Augustus, on whom Roma gazes with admiration.

Perhaps the greatest example of the effort by Augustus to spread his "gospel" comes with the *Res Gestae (Accomplishments)*. This is Augustus' own summary of his lifetime accomplishments, erected in Rome in 14 C.E. In many respects it follows the format of a descriptive series of great deeds (aretalogy) prevalent throughout the ancient world. However, this is more than a litany of the wondrous deeds of Augustus. It is a genuine propaganda product. Although the original no longer exists (probably inscribed on great bronze pillars outside his mausoleum), an inscription found in Ancyra (Turkey) provides us with the text. Evidently copies of the original were set up throughout the Empire, ensuring that even beyond death Augustus maintained control over the way in which his story was told.

Res Gestae reiterates through every portion of the text the success story of Augustus: his public offices and honors; the benefits Augustus provided through donations (money, land, grain), public works projects and spectacles; his military exploits and alliances; his influential position in Roman history; his extraordinary virtue and the recognition of being called "father of the country." It is important to see that Augustus makes it very clear that he has written this in his old age ("When I wrote this I was seventy-six years old"; par. 35). While he had consciously adopted a diffident attitude to acknowledgements of his power and influence throughout his life, he did not shy away from writing and ordering the construction of this final testimonium. In effect, Augustus attempted to keep his version of the "gospel" within the public domain. He anticipated challenges to the Roman "gospel" that would come long after he was gone. It is significant, moreover, that Augustus himself goes out of his way to note the importance of his "sanctified name" being "hymned."

*By a senate decree my name was included in the Saliar Hymn, and it
was sanctified by a law, both that I would be sacrosanct for ever, and
that, as long as I would live, the tribunician power would be mine.*
(12 B.C.E.; italics mine)

The linkage of this "sacred name" and the holding of power would not
be lost on the hearer of the *Res Gestae*. *Res Gestae* summed up all the
propaganda moves that preceded it. The image of a pious and responsible
Roman, linked to the mythic figure of Aeneas, modest in respect to the
display of power, is tied together with a catalogue of Augustus' achievements. The sheer repetition of offices and honors, donations and benefits,
victories and alliances, carries an effective rhetorical weight. The recitation of such a scroll would reinforce all that had been kept in play by the
Augustan Principate and evoke nothing less than awe.

A Dissident Voice

With such imperial clues as a cultural background, let us begin to rehear
Romans by conducting a typographical experiment. Whether in Greek
or English, modern readings of Paul are usually performed silently. One
reads left to right often without a sense of the rhetorical implications or
oral nuances of the material. I offer the following visual experiment as an
entry into re-imaging what Paul was attempting to bring off.

> and from Jesus, anointed lord.
> from God, our patron,
> benefit and peace to you
> summoned as "holy ones,"
> beloved of God,
> to all those in Rome,
> summoned by Jesus the Anointed,
> among whom you are
> for the sake of his name
> among all the heathen nations
> for a corresponding trust
> benefit and commission
> through whom we received
> "Jesus—anointed—our lord"
> from his standing up out of the dead,
> in respect to [God's] holy breath
> who was deified as "son of God" in power
> in respect to our mortal condition,
> who came from the seed of David

> about his son,
> in the sacred writings
> through his prophets
> which was announced in advance
> for the message of God,
> designated
> summoned as an emissary,
> Paul, slave of the anointed Jesus,
> (Rom 1:1–7, translation mine).

I have inverted the introduction of Romans to bring our reading to a halt. If we re-orient our usual, automatic way of reading, we can begin to catch (even in English) some sense of the majestic rhetoric of the opening of Romans. Let us begin at the bottom of the column and work up. Phrase upon phrase builds through repetition and continued declarations of accomplishment and benefit. What we have just seen in the *Res Gestae* of Augustus helps us to detect what is going on here. In his introduction to Romans Paul wants to make it quite clear how the world works. The rhetorical result is evident. The genuine ruler has been enthroned; the claims of the Roman Principate displaced. Right from the beginning of his letter Paul sets up an alternative regime.

Yet this visual experiment is somewhat misleading. If we are to "re-hear" Romans (or, to hear it "again for the first time") we need to try to detect the soundscape of these opening verses. We must remember that the letters of Paul were performed, that they resounded as waves in the ears of the listeners, most of whom were illiterate. And we need to remember that these letters were spoken in Greek. Consequently we need to spend some time among the foreign sounds of the text in order to see if we can detect any "dissonant sound," that is, any verbal clues that betray Paul's sense of the "gospel."

Here I rely on the creative contributions of Brandon Scott and Margaret Lee who have developed a method of sound-mapping ancient texts.[6] Scott and Lee have been able to determine the basic building blocks of ancient Greek sound. For an ancient speaker of Greek to deliver a persuasive speech, he would have to gather together the sounds necessary to elicit the desired response from his audience. The vision he would share with his audience would be embodied in sound. He would work through his speech, testing the way the sound patterns worked together. In many

---

6. Bernard Brandon Scott and Margaret Elen Lee, *What They Heard: Sound and Meaning in Ancient Texts* (Santa Rosa, CA: Polebridge, forthcoming).

respects the invention of an ancient speech was similar to the art of weaving, where sounds were woven like strands of cloth.

The ancients identified the building blocks of a Greek sentence as a colon (basic sense and sound group) and period (the fully sounded sentence). A period is thus composed of cola. In Rom 1:1–7 we find that this extended sentence is actually a well-crafted period (fully wrought sentence) with a multiple cola (basic sound and sense structures). One can break down Rom 1:1–7 in the following way:

Period with 5 cola: Rom 1:1–7

1 *Paulos doulos christou Iēsou*	1 Paul, slave of the anointed Jesus
klētos apostolos	summoned as an emissary
aphōrismenos eis euangelion theou	designated for the message of God
2 *ho proepēggeilato*	2 which was announced in advance
dia tōn prophētōn autou	through his prophets
en graphais hagiais	in the sacred writings
peri tou huiou autou	about his son
3 *tou genomenou ek spermatos Dauid*	3 who came from the seed of David
kata sarka	in respect to our mortal condition
tou horisthentos huiou theou en dunamei	who was deified as "son of God" in power
kata pneuma hagiōsunēs	in respect to God's holy breath
ex anastaseōs nekrōn	from his standing up out of the dead
4 *Iēsou christou tou kuriou hēmōn*	4 Jesus—anointed—our lord
di hou elabomen	through whom we received
charin kai apostolēn	benefit and commission
eis hupakoēn pisteōs	for a corresponding trust
en pasin tois ethnesin	among all the heathen nations
huper tou onomatos autou	for the sake of his name
5 *en hois este kai humeis*	5 among whom you are
klētoi Iēsou christou	summoned by Jesus the anointed
pasin tois ousin en Rhomē	to all those in Rome
agapētois theou	beloved of God
klētois hagiois	summoned as "holy ones,"
charis humin kai eirēnē	benefit and peace to you
apo theou patros hēmōn	from God, our patron,
kai kuriou Iēsou christou	and from Jesus, anointed lord.
	(translation mine)

We can see that Rom 1:1–7 is an extended period that has five cola. Sound repetitions within the cola help the hearer to make significant connections. In colon 1, *os* is associated with Paul and how he described himself.

The *os* sound related to Paul is matched by the *ois* sound associated with the addressed Roman communities in colon 5. Both Paul and the communities are described having divine roles and destinies.

In colon 1, the *ou* sound also emerges, and is associated with Jesus, the anointed and God (see also cola 2 and 3). This sound is echoed at the end of colon 5 ("From God our patron and from Jesus, anointed lord"). "Jesus Anointed" thus functions chiastically[7] at the beginning and end (cola 1, 5).

In colon 4 we have the titled name of Jesus ("Jesus–anointed–our lord!") at the beginning of the colon and at the end ("for the sake of his name"), forming another chiasm. The chiasm nicely embraces Paul's mission and the response by those who hear the message. Following on the triumphant apotheosis of colon 3, the declaration "Jesus–anointed–our lord!" functions as an acclamation. Such an acclamation would have been echoed, either in word or song, in the Roman communities of faith.

The style of this period is what Scott and Lee acknowledge as "somewhat mixed," employing both an austere style (short, abrupt cola: 1, and 5) and a polished style (cola 2, 3, and 4), with quite elegant, balanced parallelisms, repetitions. Scott and Lee have noted that works composed of short cola were deemed suitable for noble, authoritative speech.[8] Combined with the polished style of cola 2, 3, and 4, it produces overall a blended style that is both authoritative and polished. This is seen as the pinnacle of literary efforts.[9]

What do these technical comments yield for our understanding of Paul's efforts? By constructing an introduction that achieves what the ancients considered a "polished" style, Paul has attempted to present a sound pattern that would be taken seriously as an elevated piece. The letter to the Romans has entered into competition with the elegant sounds of the empire. Such formality of speech would represent an intention to

---

7. A chiasm was a well known and appreciated figure of speech. It formed a X (*chi*), where the first part reflected the last part (often the fourth), and the second part reflected the third: thus A, B, B', A'. Such an imaginative pattern helped structure the sound patterns and aided memorization. Further, audiences appreciated an extended sentence that could reflect against itself through sound and images, and thereby keep the sound in play. For Paul, to construct such a chiasm meant that he wanted to make an impression upon his audience, an imprint that could be recalled with relish.

8. Scott and Lee, *What They Heard*, 103.

9. Ibid., 101.

demonstrate that the subject matter of the discourse was on equal (or greater) footing with imperial claims.

Commentators on Romans have noted that Paul's opening greatly differs from his other letter openings (1 Thess 1:1; Gal 1:1–5; 1 Cor 1:1–3; 2 Cor 1:1–2; 2 Cor 2:14–16?; Phil 1:1–2; Phlm 1–3), both in length and elegance. It is not simply the case, however, that Paul was trying to impress an unfamiliar audience. The images, sounds, and language go beyond the attempt to make a good impression. If we recall that such sounds would echo within the very heart of the Empire, we get the distinct impression that these sounds would have been heard as fundamentally dissonant and treasonous. Not only does Jesus' earthly lineage have royal ties (Colon 3); the third colon also plays upon the imperial apotheosis. Jesus has been "deified as 'son of God' in power." His name ("Jesus–anointed–our lord!") is acclaimed, just as Augustus' name was hymned, and echoes from Paul's lips to those who call on this name with "corresponding trust" (see Rom 10:13 below). Furthermore, all nations have been "summoned" to respond (Rom 16:26).[10] Thus, we can see in these opening words that Paul is establishing himself as an emissary in grandiloquent terms. He represents a new and alternative regime and his rhetoric matches his mission. The performance of this letter opening would have offered to the Roman communities the opportunity to become co-conspirators with Paul in acknowledging that a regime change had occurred and that they were acclaiming the true ruler of the universe. Paul's *euangelion* (1:16) is thus a dynamic communication overturning the world itself.

Universal Appeal

If we then turn to Rom 10:4–13,[11] we can detect more of the Pauline dissonance. In the midst of Paul's discussion of the situation and fate of his

10. *Eis hupakoēn pisteōs* does not simply mean "to obey" but to respond out of confidence and loyalty to the worldwide summons.

11. In an earlier article ("A Re-Hearing of Romans 10:1–15," *Semeia* 65 [1994] 109–27) I have argued that this classic location of the oral hermeneutics of sound (so termed by Werner Kelber) must be understood within the power issues of the day. Paul was playing upon the utopian dreams and desires of the first century in declaring that genuine access to ultimate power was within the grasp of his listeners. What I did not consider directly was the imperial echo chamber in which these words of Paul swirled. Although I distinguished the utopian strains of Paul and Philo, I did not throw into relief what affect Rom 10: 4–13 would have upon an audience quite familiar with imperial propaganda.

people, he comes right to the nub of the argument: "Remember: the point of the tradition is seen in God's anointed, which is to make acceptance by God available to all those who trust (as Jesus did)" (10:4, Scholars Version).

Paul contrasts two ways of being in fundamental relationship with God. There is "acceptance" that comes through the tradition *(nomos)* and there is the acceptance that comes from having the confident reliance like that of Jesus.[12] Paul personifies this acceptance based on trust (Rom 10:6–8) as the female voice of *Dikaiosunē*, who speaks the words of Deut 30:12–14.[13]

But the acceptance based on trust says,	Personification
"Don't tell yourself, 'Who will go up to heaven?	Deut spoken by *Dikaiosunē*
(that is, to bring down God's anointed),	Interpretation by *Dikaiosunē*
[7]or 'Who will go down to the abyss?'	Deut spoken by *Dikaiosunē*
(that is, to bring God's anointed up from among the dead)."	Interpretation by *Dikaiosunē*
[8]Rather, what does she say?	Personification
"The message is right there, in your mouth and in your heart	Deut spoken by *Dikaiosunē*
(that is, the message of total trust we are preaching)."	Interpretation by *Dikaiosunē*

God's acceptance (*dikaiosunē*) comes as near as the heart itself and permeates the believer as a sound within. Access to the one who bestows universal benefits (that is, the ultimate patron) is no farther away than

12. In recent Pauline scholarship, the more traditional understanding of "faith in Jesus" has been challenged seriously by the notion of the "trust like Jesus." In other words, followers were exhorted not to focus their trust on Jesus but to trust God just as Jesus did. For the major critical turning point in the discussion see Richard B. Hays, *The Faith of Jesus Christ: The Narrative Substructure of Galatians 3:1—4:11*, 2d ed. The Biblical Resource Series (Grand Rapids: Eerdmans, 2001).

13. Here we must recognize the use of personification where the powers that condition existence are given a voice. For more on this see my *Spirit and Letter in Paul* (Lewiston, NY: Mellen, 1996) 174–77. Among other points, I note how Teles in the Cynic tradition personifies poverty in an attempt to get his audience to give up their assumption that poverty is the reason for their condition. Paul uses personification to great effect in his letters (e.g., in 1 Cor 12:12–26 he even personifies body parts).

the use of one's lips and heart. Speaking the acclamation of Jesus as "lord" (*kurios*) echoes the message that has entered into the person's heart ("God raised Jesus from among the dead"). The effect of these "sounds" is to stir up the memories and liturgical actions of the communities. This is similar to the way contemporary preachers "play to their audience" by using words that strike deeply within the audience. Singers, too, through a simple phrase can elicit enormous feelings, especially if that phrase is echoed throughout the song.[14]

Verses 11–13 make it clear that Paul is thinking along imperial lines. The universal reach of the Roman Empire meets its competition as Scripture (again in a feminine voice) utters a confident claim for universal effect. If we look again at the sound structure of vv. 11–13, we note the following:

Legei gar hē graphē	For the sacred writing says:
A **pas** *ho* **p**isteuōn ep autō ou kataischunthēsetai	A "Everyone who trusts in him will not be shamed" (Isa 28:16)
B **ou gar** *estin diastolē Ioudaiou te kai Hellēnos*	B Nor is there any social distinction between Jew and Greek—
B' **ho gar** *autos kurios* **p**antōn ploutōn eis **p**antas tous epikaloumenous auton	B' the same lord is lord of all enriching all who appeal to him.
A' **pas gar** *hos an epikalesē***tai** *to onoma kuriou* sōthēse**tai**.	A' For "everyone who appeals in the Lord's name will benefit." (Joel 3:5 LXX) (translation mine)

The repetition of sounds and the use of chiasmus (ABB'A') deliver a nicely balanced period. This rhetorical balance has a distinct political direction. Those who appeal in the lord's name will not be publicly shamed, but will benefit. The second and third cola make the universality of this regime quite evident. There is no ethnic distinction. The dream of Alexander the Great of a civilized world where there is not blood distinction takes hold.[15]

It should not be lost on the modern reader that the verb "appeal" (*epikalesētai*) means an appeal to an authority. Since this is a universal

14. The phrase "blowin' in the wind" for many conjures up not only the entire song written by Bob Dylan and made famous by Peter, Paul, and Mary but also triggers the anti-war protests in which this tune swirled.

15. See Plutarch *The Fate of Alexander, passim.*

appeal, the imperial throne becomes the point of comparison and rivalry. Paul is making it quite clear to the Roman communities that the capacity to appeal to and have contact with the "highest power" resides right in their midst; in fact, it lies in their hearts. This would contrast greatly with the imperial system where an appeal to the emperor would have to go through the expected hierarchical protocols. Further, an appeal to the emperor would not bring immediate relief. In contrast, says Paul, the transcendent realm has already entered into the life of the Roman communities through the members' trusting response. The very source of energy and cosmic dynamism is found in the very midst of these undistinguished people. There is no need for someone to have an advantage at the expense of another, since everyone equally has access to the "lord of all."

Such a different imagining of the universal benefit cycle would be another instance of contrary thinking and conspiracy against Rome. This universal acclamation, then, is in effect, a reprise of the letter's opening. When we consider the performative aspect of these words—that is, that they would be spoken in the context of worship—the subversive nature of this declaration is underscored. In acknowledging Jesus as lord (*kurios*), a contrast is established to the one who is publically declared lord throughout the imperial realm, namely, the emperor. Paul, through the voice of the sacred writing, is acting as a co-conspirator with the Roman communities against this imperial regime.

As modern readers we cannot let this revolutionary sound be lost. To confine these verses today to a solely religious understanding of the status of the exalted Jesus would miss Paul's dissident intent. It would also mean that we would miss what would have stirred those first century Roman communities to the bone. A new regime was on the ground and they were intimately engaged in this situation.

Politics in the Heart of the Empire

Having argued that Paul takes a definitive stance against the empire, I need to address what appears to be a contradictory note, namely, Romans 13:1–7.

> Everyone should respect the authority of government officials. Since the source of all authority is God, the present officials are

God's appointees. 2This means that someone who rebels against such authority is opposing what God has put in place, and those who do so will pay the consequences. 3Remember: government is a deterrent against criminals, not law-abiding citizens. If you don't want to be frightened of those with authority, then do what's right and you'll be rewarded. 4After all, that's God's servant working for your good. But if you commit a crime, then you have reason to be afraid, since the person in authority has legitimate use of force–this servant of God carries out punishment on the law-breaker. 5Therefore, it is obligatory to show proper respect, not just to avoid punishment, but also to be conscientious. 6Indeed, this is also the reason you pay taxes, since these are God's magis-trates, dedicated to this very task. 7Pay them all what they're due, to some it's taxes, to others it's tolls, to some it's respect, to others it's recognition. (Scholars Version)

Many interpreters of Paul traditionally have used this passage to maintain a theological justification for Christians' obedience to lawful authorities of any era even when those authorities horribly abuse their authority. There has been, however, a persistent "loyal opposition" to this traditional interpretation.[16] To understand Rom 13:1–7, it is important for us to situate it within the fuller context of the letter.

Romans 13:1–7 must first of all be read in light of what precedes in Rom 12:1–2. These verses throw the religio-political situation into critical review and rhetorically prepare the listener for what follows:

I beg you, my friends: offer yourselves, through God's mercy, as a living sacrifice that is dedicated and satisfying to God—a sensible kind of service. 2Don't be conformists to the culture, but develop your own way of thinking. Only then can you verify God's worthy, satisfying and ultimate intent for you. (Scholars Version)

Paul's advice is quite clear: Do not conform to the "way things are." This of course includes the way Roman propaganda says things are. It may even

16. Some interpreters have also argued that, since this passage does not reflect the apocalyptic character of Paul's language, it may well be a later insertion into the letter. Others have suggested that recent historical events, such as the expulsion of Jews from Rome under Claudius (49 C.E.) have forced Paul to modify his stance. Was Paul trying to keep the peace? Neil Elliott has quite competently reviewed the state of the issue on Rom 13:1–7 ("Romans 13:1–7 in the Context of Imperial Propaganda," in *Paul and Empire*, ed. Richard Horsley (Harrisburg, PA: Trinity, 1997) 184–204. I have elsewhere attempted to deal with what appears to be the political options open to Paul ("Insurgency in the Empire," *Forum* n.s. 5 (2002) 245–51.

entail (12:1) one's own life. Then Paul delivers further advice from within the wisdom tradition (Rom 12:18–21). Strikingly familiar to the sayings of Jesus in Matt 5:3, these remarks urge another way out of what would be the socially predictable alternative of "fight or flight."

> As much as you possibly can, make peace with everyone. 19 My friends, don't try to retaliate, leave that for God's day of wrath. Remember what's written: "Vengeance is for me, I'll do the payback, says the Lord." 20 Rather, "share food with your hungry enemies and give them a drink when thirsty. This way you will heap hot coals on them." 21 Don't be overwhelmed by evil, but overcome evil with good. (Scholars Version)

Now it is crucial to notice that this advice comes directly before Rom 13:1–6. In effect, this exhortation revises what has been seen as standard Jewish political wisdom. Wisdom 10:4 provides us with a reprise of that underlying ideology:

> The government of the earth is in the hands of the Lord, and over it he will raise up the right man for the time. (RSV)

In other words, the Jewish wisdom tradition grounds political power within the governance of God. Sirach 17:14–15 continues in the same vein:

> Over every nation he places a ruler . . . all their actions are clear as the sun to him, his eyes are ever upon their ways. (RSV)

That is clear also in Rom 13:1. In fact, Rom 13:1–7 very much can be characterized as the standard political wisdom that would have existed in Jewish synagogues throughout the Empire. But there is an important difference. The previous chapter has radicalized Rom 13:1–7, if the listener has caught on to what was advised in Rom 12:2:

> Don't be conformists to the culture, but develop your own way of thinking. Only then can you verify God's worthy, satisfying and ultimate intent for you. (Scholars Version)

Such advice does not imagine a passive response to life. On the contrary, it assumes an engaged, critical response. Thus, the listeners are advised to participate in peace-making and non-retaliation because, in effect, the wisdom reserved for rulers has already entered into the free speech of the Roman communities of the Anointed. In Rom 12:18–21 Paul urges a strategy that does not play into the game of fear and submission. One can up-end the dominating power structures. But this does not mean a mindless fury of reaction. To stand up against Rome in political array meant certain, if not immediate, defeat. The Jewish revolutionaries learned this in the First (66–73 C.E.) and Second (132–135 C.E.) Jewish Wars.[17] Rather, it means to live with the confident assurance that the energy cycle of the ancient world, whereby benefits and peace flow into life and culture, comes through the Anointed Jesus, not the Emperor. The gods of Rome no longer function as the divine patron of this benefit flow; instead, the God of Israel who raised the shamed criminal serves as the constant source of hope and life.

Concluding Remarks

From these considerations it becomes evident that Romans is not simply a theological treatise. It is genuinely political in the ancient sense of the word. For the ancients never separated the gods from politics; indeed, the gods delivered the energy and benefits that allowed humans to construct their lives together. There is thus more to this letter than what is usually construed. What this "more" is becomes clear when we take pains to hear the imperial echo chamber in which the letter was performed. Within this "surround sound" the gospel of Paul emerges as a dissonant voice, presenting an affront to the gospel of the Empire. Paul's opening remarks deliver a well-crafted revision of how the world works. This formal ambassadorial beginning would have been portrayed with grandiloquence and formality. As the performance of the letter unfolded it encouraged people still unknown to Paul[18] to make their appeal loud and strong to "Jesus—anointed—lord!" (*Iēsous christos kurios*). Through this declaration of allegiance to the alternative regime of the Anointed, Paul encouraged the Roman communities to take an active stance of non-conformity

---

17. Dewey, "Insurgency in the Empire."

18. The actual social make-up of the Roman communities is still very much a matter of dispute and conjecture. We do not know how these communities started. Some have suggested migration from the east was enough to bring this about. Moreover, the communities could well have been of mixed social status. For more on the social situation in Rome see the recent volume of Rodney Stark, *Cities of God: The Real Story of How Christianity Became an Urban Movement and Conquered Rome* (San Francisco: HarperSanFrancisco, 2006).

to the present age, by critically engaging the challenge to live as if the benefits of the universal patron were truly available to all.

In light of such remarks, one can understand very well the legends of Paul's demise. Such language would be tantamount to treason. While there are legends about Paul's beheading, it might be better to recognize that, given the lack of historical certainty, Paul ends as one of those who "disappeared" in the Empire. His words remain, an unfinished agenda, often embalmed in theological winding sheets.

A modern critical performance of Romans, however, may still bring Paul's agenda to life. If the interpreter of Paul pays close attention to the sound structure of his rhetoric and notes the letter's contrapuntal movement against the Imperial system, then even a performance in translation may catch Paul's dissident voice. If one were to incorporate light and sound together, such as using images of power and dominance (either ancient or modern), then the words delivered would take on particular undertones. Moreover, if the performer of Romans were to encourage the listeners' participation in sound and song, the raucous intent of Paul might yet shake some ground.

Questions

1. What was the character of the imperial echo chamber described in this article and what challenge does Paul offer to this imperial sound system?

2. In what different contexts does this essay identify words being spoken and heard? What is suggested about how hearing words spoken might differ from reading words?

3. In our own day, do you feel that the Paul's understanding of the gospel challenges or supports those who are in power on the global scene? In what ways do imperial gospels promise peace and prosperity today?

PART II

Story and Performance
in the Modern World

6

WHAT IS PERFORMANCE CRITICISM?

DAVID RHOADS

MOST OF US READ AND STUDY THE NEW TESTAMENT SILENTLY and in private. Or we hear it read to us as brief passages from the Bible in worship. But what if this is not at all how the early Christians encountered the writings? What if the writings of the New Testament were not what we thought they were?

For centuries, we have been treating these scriptures as "writings"— written to have a long-lasting presence in the Christian religion, written to be studied and interpreted as manuscripts, written to be broken up into lessons for worship or read privately for devotion. We have been dealing with them as if they were part of a *print* culture. But what if the writings now collected in the New Testament are the remnants of *oral events*? What if the gospels are more like transcriptions of performances by epic storytellers in the mode of Homer? What if the letters are closer in genre to rhetorical speeches? What if the *Book of Revelation* was like a script for an ancient drama? What if they are examples of "oral literature"? Actually, they are! Some are transcripts of oral performances; and others are scripts dictated or written for performance.

And this shift from print culture to oral culture changes everything. Treating the New Testament writings as oral literature is a paradigm shift that has enormous implications for the entire field of New Testament studies. These collected writings were not originally experienced as Scripture on inked pages but as oral stories and epic-like tales and speeches and drama. Each was meant to be performed, not read privately, but enacted in social settings before gatherings of people. They were most likely originally performed in their entirety, probably from memory, and not broken up into small sections. In order to gain a deeper understanding of these writings, we should try to construct what the original performance events were like. It means that we should fundamentally revise our traditional methods in order to study these "writings" in the context of the oral cultures of early Christianity. It means that we need to perform these writings in our classrooms and in our churches as a means to gain some sense of the original experience of the New Testament traditions.

After about twenty centuries, we are beginning to recover something that has been lost, eclipsed from the experience of the church and from the experience of Christians—namely, the sacred art of telling biblical traditions. Such tradition-telling was widespread in early Christianity: as informal gossip in the marketplaces or as teaching in the home or as storytelling in ordinary conversation when recalling these traditions.[1] There were also formal opportunities in marketplaces and open spaces between villages and house churches and synagogues and other gathering places for people to recount lengthier oral pieces that now comprise the New Testament. The gospels Matthew, Mark, Luke, and John, along with the Acts of the Apostles and the book of Revelation, were probably each told in their entirety. The same was true for the epistles; they were letter-speeches dictated to be performed as a whole before the churches to which they were addressed. The writings now collected in the New Testament were originally either told and then retold, each time to the same audience or to new audiences as the writings (and the performers) circulated from one venue to another. And, again, they were probably told in their entirety, because, after all, if you had heard only part of any one of these writings and not the whole, you would likely have misunderstood it.

The First Century as an Oral Culture

Orality studies are teaching us a great deal about the societies of the ancient Mediterranean world as oral cultures.[2] It is likely that only about 5

1. See the essays by Holly E. Hearon and Joanna Dewey in this volume. See also Hearon, *The Mary Magdalene Tradition: Witness and Counter-Witness in Early Christian Communities* (Collegeville, MN: Liturgical, 2004).

2. See, for example, Susan Niditch, *Oral World and Written Word* (Louisville: Westminster John Knox, 1996); Walter Ong, *Orality and Literacy* (London: Routledge, 1988); Jonathan Draper, *Orality, Literacy, and Colonialism in Antiquity* (Atlanta: Society

percent of the people—mostly wealthy elites—were able to read or write. The overwhelming 95 percent of the people were non-literate peasants or urban dwellers who experienced everything they learned aurally. Everything they learned and knew, they learned by word of mouth. In the collectivist cultures of the first century, there was little opportunity for privacy for most people. People lived together as large nuclear or extended families, houses were open to neighbors, and marketplaces were centers of social interaction. Life was communal life. There was no individualism as we know it today. The identity of individuals came as part of their collective identity. People were always with other people, and what one person knew everybody knew. Knowledge was social knowledge because everybody talked with everybody else and everybody told stories. Memory was social memory. Imagine never having a newspaper or book or anything else written that you could access, let alone radio, television or the internet. What you would know would be what you collectively knew as a family and a village and a community. In an oral culture, all language—words and proverbs and stories and letters—were always embodied; that is, for almost everyone there was no experience of impersonal writing on a scroll unassociated with a person. In an oral culture, life was overwhelmingly relational and social.

In such a culture, people were adept at remembering what they heard, in part because people were accustomed and trained to remember what they heard. Furthermore, in an oral culture, people remembered because there were sophisticated forms for creating memorable speech. People thought about how they talked, so that it could be easily remembered—with proverbs and parables and words that had a ring to them and stories and all kinds of teachings in which words were made to sound right and good. Also, in an oral culture, words were understood to have power. When you think about the words in the early church, many of them are performative words, words that performed a healing or exorcised a demon or pronounced a blessing. Words were actions that had an impact meant to change people—change the way people think or relate or act or imagine the world. Such words were memorable words.

---

of Biblical Literature, 2004). Orality critics seek to understand from oral cultures—ancient and modern—the ethos of orality, the impact of writing in different cultures, the responsibilities and practices of tradents, the dynamics of social memory, the power dimensions of oral/written communication, and the gender dimensions of orality.

In the oral cultures of the first century, writing was present but rare, and reading was limited. Writing was done on scrolls or paper made of papyrus reeds pressed together. The scrolls and the writing implements were expensive. The leisure time and the resources to learn how to make letter characters were available almost exclusively to the five percent of elites (and to their slaves and retainers who may have written/read manuscripts for them). Even some who knew how to read may not have known how to write. And some scribes probably could copy letters without knowing what they meant.

On the scrolls, the letters were placed one after another without punctuation and without spaces between words. Even when there was writing, that writing was not done for its own sake. Rather, orality remained primary, and writing was secondary and served the needs of orality. People wrote the letter characters on a scroll to provoke the memory of the sounds that they and others might need as aids to remembering. Eventually, people also wrote to enable oral stories and letters to be transferred from one city or region to another.

The New Testament Writings in an Oral Culture

The Gospel of Mark was probably composed orally and performed many times before it was transcribed at some point in its performance life. Other gospels may have developed the same way. Or a gospel may have been written before it was performed but certainly with the expectation and purpose that it would be performed—that was the whole point. Paul probably composed his letters mentally or in conversation and dictated them orally to be written down by a scribe. Then Paul would send the letter with an emissary who probably would have heard Paul dictate it and who would have gotten instructions from Paul about how it should be performed. It is likely the emissary memorized the letter and performed it with little reference to the scroll itself, perhaps even expanding on the letter at the direction of the sender. Because scrolls were cumbersome and words were compressed together, a reader would have had to know the contents extremely well to "read" it. The scroll may have been held closed in one hand as a sign of authority. But it was most likely not consulted during a performance. The same would be true for all the other letters in the New Testament.

When people referred to the Gospel of Mark (not so-called in the first century) or a letter of Paul, they were not referring to a scroll much less a book. Rather, they were referring to the performances they had experienced! In the first century, the contents of the New Testament writings were not encountered by the overwhelming majority as writing on a scroll. Rather, they were embodied in a performer at a communal event.

So, is the Bible what we have in print? Or is it the stories and speeches that were performed, of which our Bible contains the remnants? In this regard, the written gospels and the letters may be seen as records of/for oral performances. Dennis Dewey has likened the print in the Bible to a fossil. Just as a fossil is a trace record of what was once a living creature, so the New Testament writings are trace records of live performances in the first century. We can get some clues to the live performances from the writings themselves. For example, they contain language that reflects features of oral storytelling and memorable speech. The texts reflect the performer's use of voice when, for example, the text says that someone "shouted." They reflect gestures used in performance when the writings depict, say, the laying on of hands. The texts may imply facial expressions when there is irony or amazement. They also suggest movement for the performer as characters go from place to place in the story. To a limited extent, then, we may be able to infer from the "fossil writings" something of what an original live performance may have been like.

Again, the oral performance was primary; the manuscript was not. Imagine that you heard a lively telling of the story of Paul's conversion and that your aural hearing of it was the only way to access that story. As a modern, literate person you would want someone to make a transcript of what was said so you could read it. However, when you read the script, you might say, "That's a nice script, but so much is lost. It's not the same as hearing the story told by someone." The story is in the lively telling of it. Or imagine you were to get a transcript from a performance at Comedy Central; you would be sadly disappointed. It would not be nearly as funny or as interesting as the performance itself, because you would not have the inflections and the gestures and the facial expressions and the body posture and the timing and everything else that goes into a live performance.

Therefore, the writings we have in the New Testament are examples of "performance literature," that is, literature that was meant for performance—no less than music, no less than theater, no less than oral interpretation of literature. Can you imagine a musicologist spending years sitting in libraries looking at scores but never hearing the music performed? Can you imagine theater critics studying scripts but never seeing the performance of a play? Can you imagine how we biblical scholars have studied these texts for centuries without hearing them performed as stories and speeches? Can we imagine biblical scholars themselves performing these writings? The meaning of a text comes to bear at the point where it is performed. Performers are figuring out the range of meanings for these texts and seeking to embody them. That is what we scholars are challenged to do. That is what we Christians are challenged to do. The act of performance is the reason for scripts!

Biblical Performance Criticism

Thus there is a gap in New Testament studies. There is something missing in our study of early Christianity, namely, the oral/aural events in which early Christian writings were performed before a communal audience. There are many studies now emerging to help fill this gap. I propose to designate the emerging biblical discipline as "performance criticism."[3] Biblical performance criticism is not one more methodology added on to other methodologies. Rather, it is a paradigm shift from print medium to oral medium that has implications for the entire enterprise of New Testament studies.[4] New methodologies and the transformation of traditional methodologies are needed to address this media shift in the biblical writings.

How might we formulate performance criticism? What processes might be developed that would lead to an understanding of the phenomenon of performance in early Christianity? I would like to suggest three approaches: 1) One approach is to construct in imagination one or more performative events for each particular writing and then study the writing with those scenarios in mind. 2) The second approach is to reorient the methods by which we study the New Testament in light of the oral dimensions of the writings. 3) The third approach is to do performances

---

3. For more information, see David Rhoads, "Performance Criticism: An Emerging Methodology in Second Testament Studies," Part I and Part II, *BTB* 36 (2006) 118–33; 164–84.

4. See the chapter by Robert Fowler in this volume. See also J. A. Loubser, *Orality and Manuscript Culture in the Bible* (Stellenbosch, South Africa: Sun, 2007).

of these texts in our primary languages as means to get in touch with the performative dimensions of these writings in their original contexts.

Imagining a Performative Event

I am focusing here primarily on public performances of whole New Testament writings for gathered groups, rather than on informal storytelling of brief traditions. The performative event includes the act of performing, the performer, the audience, the location, the cultural/historical circumstances, and the implied rhetorical impact on the audience. One purpose of performance criticism is to ask: How do all these factors combine to suggest a range of meanings and potential rhetorical impacts?

The Act of Performing

The event of a performance is much more than the oral dimensions. It includes intonation, movements, gestures, pace, facial expressions, postures, the spatial relationships of the imagined characters, the temporal development of the story in progressive events displayed on stage, and much more. Nor can we ignore the sheer force of the bodily presence of the performer to evoke emotions and commitments. The composition-as-performance was not a written text but an oral presentation embodied in the performance. When we imagine first century scenarios, we need to imagine the stories and letter-speeches as being very expressive and emotional, filled with drama in voice and gesture and physical movement. We need to scour ancient art and literature for depictions and directions and descriptions of ancient performances done by rhetoricians and storytellers and dramatists. We need to look at each writing to discover clues in the writing itself as to how such performances may have been enacted.[5]

The Performer

The performer is the medium that bears the potential meanings and impacts of the story upon the audience in a particular context. In the performance of a narrative, the performer is acting out the characters and events of the story. In the performance of a letter, the performer is

5. See Whitney Shiner, *Proclaiming the Gospel: First-Century Performance of Mark* (Harrisburg, PA: Trinity, 2003); and William Shiell, *Reading Acts: The Lector and the Early Christian Audience*, Biblical Interpretation Series 70 (Boston: Brill Academic, 2004).

personifying the dynamics of the argument that is being presented. The early Christians had no un-embodied experiences of the stories or letters. The performer, as medium, was always an integral dimension of the composition. On a faith level, the performer of these particular writings needed to embody the values, beliefs, and actions enjoined by the story/letter being performed, because the performer was seeking to have the values and beliefs of the story embodied in turn in the actions and dynamics of the communal life of the audience. The social location of the performer made a difference: male, female, Judean, Gentile, Roman, peasant, elite, soldier, or slave. We can imagine different people doing different performances of a writing and imagine how the performance may have been received in each case.

The Audience

The audience was communal, and the reception of a performance was communal. Such an audience might collectively have a variety of emotional and ideological responses to the values, beliefs, arguments, and depictions presented. Whitney Shiner argues that audiences of gospels and letters may have cheered, jeered, clapped, hooted, laughed, wept, gasped, shouted, heckled, given various verbal responses of acclamation, and engaged in other forms of interruption.[6] We might imagine such responses by different groups in the audience at various points in a performance. Furthermore, performance generates community. The shared event gives the audience an experience of solidarity.

Social location was crucial to the response of ancient audiences, especially audiences from divergent cultures—a Gentile audience compared to a Judean one, or an audience in Asia Minor compared to one in Palestine or Rome, or an urban audience in contrast to a rural audience. At the same time, a single audience may have included people from diverse social locations. We may do well to imagine how peasants and elites, slaves and masters, women and men, Pharisees and Sadducees, Judeans and Romans, as well as others in an audience might have experienced a particular writing.

---

6. Shiner, *Proclaiming the Gospel*, 143–90.

The Location

The material context makes a difference in performance. Contexts raise expectations of what does or does not happen in a particular place. As such, different places foster or inhibit certain audience responses. Ancient settings for performance included synagogues, a village marketplace, an ancient theater, a house, and open spaces between villages. Location shaped the make-up of an audience that gathered for a performance. We might imagine a particular writing in diverse locations and seek to determine what difference the place might make.

The Socio-Historical Circumstances

We need to imagine these differing audiences hearing a composition-in-performance under divergent circumstance—persecution, conflict, oppression, war, social unrest, poverty, prosperity, and so on. True, we have been saying the same things about the crucial importance of context for interpreting the New Testament as written documents. However, imagining specific socio-historical circumstances in the context of an imagined performative event transforms our understanding of "reception." We are now speaking in fresh ways about echoes and associations, about an enlivened imagination, about a richer meaning potential of a text, and about greater immediacy of experience and conflict. To do so is to speak in fresh ways about a "politics of performance."[7] For example, how might different factions in an audience react to a letter and to each other in the reception of a letter?

The Rhetorical Effect/Impact

The final factor in the dynamics of the performative event is the potential rhetorical impact upon an audience. By rhetoric, I mean the impact of the entire composition-as-performance on an audience. What is the potential impact of an oral performance upon an audience—subversion of cultural values, transformation of worldview, impulse to action, change of behavior, emotional catharsis, ethical commitment, intellectual insight, change of political perspective, re-formation of community, the generation of a new world? Put another way, what does a story or a letter lead the audience

---

7. Richard Ward, "Paul and the Politics of Performance at Corinth: A Study of 2 Corinthians 10-13," PhD. diss., Northwestern University, Evanston, IL, 1987.

to become—such that they are different people in the course of and as a result of experiencing the performance?

Conclusion

From all these elements of the performative event, we can develop distinct "audience scenarios" as a basis for interpreting each writing in the New Testament. The question for performance criticism is this: How can we find ways to analyze all these elements of the performative event together so as to transform the ways we interpret the written texts as oral literature and so as to re-configure our image of the early church?

Re-orienting New Testament Methods

The second approach of performance criticism is to reorient our methods of study in light of the oral nature of the culture and the texts of the New Testament. As we have said, recognizing the orality of the New Testament writings is a paradigm shift; in principle, it impacts all methods. The key to this reorientation is to focus on the performative event as a context to re-conceptualize all methodologies. Performance criticism is a multidisciplinary approach that then makes use of the re-oriented biblical methodologies in its work.

Traditional Historical-Critical Methods

Traditional criticisms such as textual criticism, source criticism, form criticism, and genre criticism look different in a performance context. For example, scholars are rethinking textual criticism by explaining the fluidity of the earliest manuscript traditions in light of the fluidity of oral performances and by attending to the role of "memory variants" by scribes.[8] Also, source critics are now rethinking the "literary" solutions to the synoptic problem by taking into account multiple oral origins for the sayings of Jesus, the development of traditions as oral re-compositions, the force of oral speech as a factor in recollection, and the idea that social memory involves people recalling traditions in the framework of histori-

---

8. See D. C. Parker, *The Living Text of the Gospels* (Cambridge: Cambridge University Press, 1997); David Carr, *Writing on the Tablets of the Heart: Origins of Scripture and Literature* (Oxford: Oxford University Press, 2005).

cal complexes.[9] Form and genre criticism can be re-oriented by asking how forms and genres such as parable, gospel, apocalypse, epistle, wisdom tradition, and ethical exhortation function to raise, subvert, and confirm expectations in the temporal experience of an oral performance.

Some Recent Methodologies

More recent methodologies include rhetorical criticism, narrative criticism, discourse analysis, social science analysis, and ideological criticism. You can see examples of two of these disciplines in other chapters in this book. Whitney Shiner is recovering the oral dynamics of rhetorical criticism. Scholars think many New Testament letters were oral compositions shaped by the canons of ancient rhetoric, but they have not yet dealt with the oral dimensions of the letters as speeches. Philip Ruge-Jones re-orients narrative criticism in light of the fact that narrative traditions were always embodied by a performer and received by an actual audience. A similar re-orientation transforms reader-response criticism to audience-response criticism.

Another fruitful transformation may occur with discourse analysis. Recently, discourse critics have begun to ask about the oral impact on an audience of linguistic features such as chiastic patterns, chain sentences, parallelism, word order, foregrounding and backgrounding, emphasis, elision, transitions, verbal threads, onomatopoeia, hook words, mnemonic devices, and many forms of repetition.[10] Furthermore, we can reflect on the impact of sound itself upon a hearer, such as the use of guttural sounds, alliteration, assonance, and repetition of sounds.[11] We may best be able to get at these discourse features of Greek texts by listening to them. Ideological criticism can shift its focus on texts to make explicit the power dynamics of oral performance events and to reveal whose interests

9. See, for example, James D. G. Dunn, *Jesus Remembered* (Grand Rapids: Eerdmans, 2003); and Werner H. Kelber, "Orality, Scribality, and Oral-Scribal Interfaces: Jesus—Tradition—Gospels, Review and Present State of Research." Paper presented at the SNTS conference in Halle, Germany, August 2005.

10. In regard to discourse analysis on the works of Paul, see, for example, Casey Davis, *Oral Biblical Criticism: The Influence of the Principles of Orality on the Literary Structures of Paul's Epistle to the Philippians*, Journal for the Study of the New Testament Supplements Series 172 (Sheffield: Sheffield Academic, 1999); and John Harvey, *Listening to the Text: Oral Patterning in Paul's Letters* (Grand Rapids: Baker, 1988).

11. See Margaret Dean, "The Grammar of Sound in Greek Texts: Towards a Method of Mapping the Echoes of Speech in Writing," *Australian Biblical Review* 44 (1996) 53–70.

in an audience are served by the composition and whose interests are violated, denigrated, and neglected.[12]

New Disciplines

Performance criticism can also bring into the center some new disciplines for New Testament study: speech-act theory, theater studies, performance studies in the oral interpretation of literature, and the practice of translation. Speech-act theory works well with the biblical understanding that words are actions that generate and change reality.[13] New Testament study also has much to learn from theater studies about the dramatic dynamics of the biblical narratives.[14] And performance studies in the oral interpretation of literature can enable us to discern performative dynamics of the New Testament texts that we might not otherwise notice.[15] The art and practice of translation is also a fruitful area for re-orientation as scholars translate from orality to orality, seeking to discern the original oral dimensions of the biblical writings and to preserve them in dynamic translations for performance in contemporary oral cultures.[16]

Summary

It should be clear that performance criticism must be seen as a discrete discipline in its own right so as to be able to focus on the event of performance. At the same time, when one sees the magnitude and diversity of the subjects and methods of performance criticism, one can see how important it is that this discipline be multifaceted and that it partner with many fields of biblical study.

---

12. See the chapter in this volume by Arthur Dewey.

13. Richard Briggs, *Words in Action: Speech-Act Theory and Biblical Interpretation* (Edinburgh: T. & T. Clark, 2001).

14. Shimon Levy, *The Bible as Theatre* (Brighton: Sussex Academic, 2000).

15. See below, note 18.

16. James Maxey, "Bible Translation as Contextualization: The Role of Oral Performance in New Testament and African Contexts." PhD. diss., Lutheran School of Theology at Chicago, 2008.

Performing as a Method of Interpretation

Many of us contributing to this volume have been performing biblical selections for many years, including whole gospels, letters, and the book of Revelation. And we have been teaching our students to learn and perform stories and other traditions from the Bible. These experiences have been an important part of our efforts to interpret the New Testament writings in their ancient contexts.[17]

David Rhoads caught in the act of performance[18]

We can never recover a first-century performative event, but we can experiment with twenty-first-century performances as a way to help us understand the meaning and rhetoric of the biblical texts in their historical context. Again, this approach involves a media shift. Hearing the

17. See the chapters in this volume by Dennis Dewey, Marty Steussy, and Richard Swanson. See also Thomas E. Boomershine, *Story Journey: An Invitation to the Gospel as Storytelling* (Nashville: Abingdon, 1988).

18. Photo by Jan Boden, Director of Communications and Marketing at the Lutheran School of Theology at Chicago. Used by permission.

New Testament places the interpreter in a different medium relationship with the text from the traditional print medium. Performing the text goes further, enabling the interpreter to become the voice and embodiment of the narrative or letter. If the goal of interpretation is to understand a New Testament writing in its ancient context, contemporary performing can open us exegetes to many dynamics of the text that we might otherwise ignore or misunderstand.

The Performer's Approach

Simply reading the text aloud does not do it; this simply replicates in public the act of reading in private. With reading, there is no immediacy, no liveliness, and no interactive relationship with the audience. To get into interpretation, it is necessary to perform for an audience without depending on a script.

I have found several decisions about performing that serve me well as an interpreter. I recommend performing in your first language and doing a word for word memorization as the best way to interpret. Memorization leads you to notice every detail of the text. I also suggest using contemporary techniques of oral interpretation that are familiar to contemporary audiences, rather than trying to imitate an ancient means of performing.

As you memorize, you get the words off the page and into the realm of sound. Then you imagine the scene before you and tell what you are seeing in imagination. When you perform, you not only tell about the scene, you show it. When you perform a story, you take on the voice and perspective of the narrator. When you perform a letter, you assume the voice of the composer of the letter and imagine the audience to be the recipients.[19] In these ways, you will be placing yourself as an interpreter in the same relationship to the traditions that the ancient performer had.

In so doing, the performer overcomes an atomistic approach to the text. The performer becomes immersed in the "narrative world" of a gospel or a letter, imagining its characters, settings, and events, its past and future, its cosmology of space and time, its cultural dynamics, and its

---

19. See Charlotte Lee and Frank Galati, *Oral Interpretation*, 7th ed. (Boston: Houghton Mifflin, 1977, 1987); Ronald Pelias, *Performance Studies: The Interpretation of Aesthetic Texts* (New York: St. Martin's, 1992); and Leland Roloff, *The Perception and Evocation of Literature* (Glenview, IL: Scott, Foresman, 1973).

socio-political realities—all from the standards and beliefs of the narrator or the composer. Entering this world is like walking through an imaginary door into a different reality or imaginatively crossing a border into another culture. The world of the text becomes three-dimensional. This experience amplifies the interpreter's experience of the text.

The role of the performer, then, is not just to memorize and repeat the text. The performer acts it out. The performer adds sounds, gestures, facial expressions, glances, pace, pauses, pitch, volume, movement, posture, body language, proximity to audience, and so on. As we have suggested, the text itself can serve as a "script" for performance. In the descriptions of events and by dint of language, the texts contain "stage directions" for the performer's enactment. These stage directions are not simply illustrative or added on. They are an integral and indispensable part of the script-in-performance. Attending to these details not only assists in performing, it also leads us as interpreters to notice facets in the text we might otherwise overlook.

Dynamics of Performing

The performer brings the characters to life—each with their own attitudes, emotions, physical expressions, and vocal traits. The narrator takes on the distinct role of each of the characters as they speak and act in the narrative by personifying them. As such, personification is a form of interpretation. The characters come to life in performance, however briefly. By personifying the sender of a letter or an apocalypse, the performer becomes aware of certain dynamics of the sender—their personal appeals (Galatians and Philemon), self-descriptions (2 Corinthians), depictions of the audience and other characters (Philippians), along with descriptions of events and emotions (Revelation). Attending to characterization in performance sharpens our interpretive awareness of many aspects of the text—diverse points of view, the dynamics and course of conflicts, the major and minor themes, and the potential rhetorical impacts.

There are two additional features of performing that assist with interpretation: subtext and non-verbal communications. The subtext refers to the message that the performer gives in the *way* a line is delivered. This is a level of interpretation largely unexplored in biblical studies, because silent reading in print does not require one to address the issue of subtext. All performers have to decide what message or impact they will convey by *how* they say each and every line with certain inflections and intonations. It is a common exercise in oral interpretation to take a simple line and attempt to say the same line in as many different ways as possible by changing the subtext with the use of tone, volume, pitch, pace, accentuation, and so on. For example, the Markan Jesus says to the disciples, "Don't you understand yet?" In so doing, is he being patient or impatient or ironic or sarcastic? The performer must choose. In performance, subtext is unavoidable, since the performer must say each line in some way.[20] As such, the performer must infer the subtext from the text and/or supply it to the text, just as punctuation is supplied by interpreters to make sense of an ancient manuscript.[21]

Nonverbal expressions also convey the subtext. Nonverbal communication includes such things as gestures, posture, and facial expressions. Again, non-verbal communications do not just reinforce or illustrate verbal communication; rather, they are an integral part of the verbal communication itself, and they often determine its meaning. When Paul tells the Philippians that he accepts the hardships on him caused by others who are preaching while he is in prison, the passage will mean different things with a sigh or a shrug or a smile. The experience of supplying nonverbal expression in performance is integral to our interpretive efforts to grasp the possible meanings and the possible rhetorical impacts in antiquity.

Finally, all of these dynamics of performance bring to the fore both the emotional force and the humor of a text as means of persuasion. The emotive dimensions of a text are an integral and indispensable means of conveying its meaning and transformative power. For example, how can one portray the death of Jesus without powerful emotions? And there is humor in texts that performers can bring out in the act of performing. We may infer the potential for humor in the text from such features as irony, contrasts, plays on words, misunderstandings, and revealing insights into human nature. The dialogues of misunderstanding in the Gospel of John—in which Jesus and other characters talk past each other with

20. For more on this technique, see Richard W. Swanson, *Provoking the Gospel: Methods to Embody Biblical Storytelling through Drama* (Cleveland: Pilgrim, 2004) along with his lectionary commentaries: *Provoking the Gospel of Matthew* (Cleveland: Pilgrim, 2007); *Provoking the Gospel of Mark* (Cleveland: Pilgrim, 2005); *Provoking the Gospel of Luke* (Cleveland: Pilgrim, 2006); *Provoking the Gospel of John* (Cleveland: Pilgrim, forthcoming).

21. This analogy was suggested to me by storyteller Pam Faro.

puns and plays on words—are quite humorous. Both emotion and humor engender transformation, generate audience solidarity, and enhance memory. Both are critical in interpretation.

Rhetoric and Audience

There is no better way to be in touch with the rhetorical impact upon an audience than to perform it to a live audience. Silent reading may eclipse the rhetorical impact. Silent readers tend to focus upon what the text *means* and neglect what the text *does* in performance. Clearly the text is more powerful in performance than in reading; so performing offers a better chance to be in touch with the rhetorical dynamics. My own experience of performing has convinced me that we need to broaden our conception of the potential impact that a narrative or a letter may have on hearers. Persuading the audience to embrace a certain viewpoint or take a certain action may be only the beginning of the possibilities. For example, Mark does not just give people the reasons not to be paralyzed by fear; rather, the rhetorical dynamic of the gospel seeks to evoke in the audience the capacity to be faithful in the face of threat. Matthew does not just condemn hypocrisy; his sayings serve to expose/reveal it in the audience. John does not just talk about eternal life; he seeks to evoke the experience of it in the audience. The letter of Philemon does not just lead Philemon to take a certain action; the letter seeks to effect the transformation of relationships in the whole community from hierarchy to mutuality. The composer of the epistle of James does not just promote a certain viewpoint to a disengaged reader; he wants to generate in the hearers the ability to be wise in their context.

Conclusion

The purpose of performance criticism is to identify an emerging methodology in New Testament studies as a means to address the neglected dimension of performance in early Christianity and to formulate some organizing principles and procedures.[22] To do this, we need to clarify the dynamics of performative events. In addition, new methodologies and the re-orientation of traditional methodologies are needed to address the

22. Consult an internet site designed to trace the developments in Biblical performance criticism (www.biblicalperformancecriticism.org).

paradigm shift about the biblical writings in light of the orality of early Christianity and of the New Testament writings. Finally, contemporary performing can help us understand the dynamics of performance. There is much to be done. Therefore, this is just the beginning of a conversation to which many people will contribute.

Questions and Exercises

1. What does it mean to say that "the orality of the biblical writings creates a paradigm shift in biblical studies"? Do you agree?

2. What do you think of the idea of "performance criticism" as a way to address the oral dimensions of New Testament writings? How might you formulate it differently?

3. Invite several people in your group to memorize and perform a story about Jesus or a parable of Jesus. Or have people memorize and perform different miracle stories or conflict stories from one of the gospels. Afterward, invite hearers in the group to reflect on their experience. Then invite the performers to reflect on their experience. Discuss the ways in which these experiences might foster an understanding of these stories in their ancient context.

4. Invite one or more people in your group to memorize and perform Paul's letter to Philemon. Designate each person in the group to represent in imagination different people mentioned in the letter as well as people in Philemon's community who come from different social locations. After the performance(s), discuss the letter from the perspective of the different characters and their various social locations.

7

THE WORD HEARD

How Hearing a Text Differs from Reading One

Philip Ruge-Jones

Introduction

IN THE SPRING OF 2008 I HAD THE OPPORTUNITY TO TEACH a course on the Gospel of Mark that involved fifteen students reading the Gospel of Mark, studying what others have said about it, and reporting to each other their findings. The unique aspect of this course was that the key project was not a written paper but a two-hour-long public performance of the entire gospel from memory by the students. Each of them had to learn the equivalent of one chapter of Mark's gospel and be ready to present it to a gathering of other students, family members, and people of the larger community.[1] The course was exciting for students and professor alike, and the final performance has left its mark on us all. In this chapter, I will lay out the motivation for using performance, and explain the process followed by the students to prepare for the storytelling evening. Finally I will explore what was learned from hearing the story in performance rather than read silently. What difference does the media experience make?

---

1. The students in this class were Jessica Adame, William Ryan Brown, Wes Cain, Adam J. Costa, Chris Crowder, Andrew P. Dietzel, Brad Eubanks, Stuart Hendricksen, Jonathan Lys, Jessica Matlack, Kiesha Priem, Amanda Schnelle, Paul Theiss, Anna Troy, and Brittany Wheeler.

Why Perform the Gospel?

The primary reason this class sought to perform Mark's Gospel has to do with its original media setting. The Gospel of Mark had its beginnings in a context thoroughly immersed in oral communication. A growing number of scholars believe that this gospel was performed multiple times before it was ever written down. People experienced it as a lively, engaged performance. This is evident from the opening lines of Mark's Gospel: "The beginning of the good news of Jesus the anointed one, the son of God" (1:1).[2] The word for good news or gospel refers to an act of oral proclamation. It means an announcement. This word can also relate to the messenger of good news. Thomas Boomershine notes that the Greek word is derived from a Latin one that means "a tale whose telling had power."[3] The Gospel of Mark was not first and foremost ink on paper, but a story told with energy and passion.

The world in which that first line of Mark was spoken was a world immersed in oral expression. People in the ancient world regularly would listen to long stories and other forms of speech for hours on end. The Gospel of Mark takes about two hours to perform which sounds to us like a long time to sit and listen, but people in the ancient world often listened to proclamation for such extensive periods. Oral performance took place for the purposes of entertainment, education, and formation. This was true when Jewish people gathered in synagogues to hear the Word of the Lord in worship. But it was just as true in the culture of the Roman Empire that engulfed Jesus and his people. As Whitney Shiner makes clear throughout his work, the Roman world preferred oral performance and its liveliness to "the dead written letter . . ."[4] (See both Whitney Shiner and Holly Hearon's chapters in this book.)

Those becoming followers of Jesus encountered stories in performance for a basic reason: they could not read. Generous estimates of literacy in the ancient world believe ten percent could read at some level.

2. The translations in this chapter are taken with some modification from David Rhoads, Joanna Dewey, and Donald Michie, *Mark as Story: An Introduction to the Narrative of a Gospel,* 2d ed. (Minneapolis: Fortress, 1999) 8–38.

3. Thomas E. Boomershine, *Story Journey: An Invitation to the Gospel as Storytelling* (Nashville: Abingdon, 1988) 16.

4. Whitney Shiner, "Memory Technology and the Composition of Mark," in *Performing the Gospel: Orality, Memory, and Mark,* ed. Richard A. Horsley, Jonathan A. Draper, and John Miles Foley (Minneapolis: Fortress, 2006) 147.

Among people in the land where Jesus lived the percentage might have been only a third of this larger number.[5] So if ninety-seven out of one hundred people were to encounter the story of Jesus, they would have to do so through hearing it rather than reading it. The form of Mark itself conforms to the style of performance: connected episodes, oral structures in the plot, the use of repetition. Based on these clues, Joanna Dewey concludes that this book was composed in performance, repeatedly experienced in performance, and had a life of its own even after someone wrote it down.[6]

Taking the Text to Heart

Given the confidence with which we can speak of the performance origins of Mark's gospel, fifteen students and I embarked on a journey into this story in order to find out what could be revealed about it through performance. In order to understand how those performance dynamics took place in the final staging of the story, it is helpful to understand the journey that took us there.[7]

In some ways this academic course was like any other at a university. We read common textbooks, including a short commentary on Mark's gospel,[8] a guide to effective storytelling,[9] and Boomershine's book on biblical storytelling.[10] We had quizzes to make sure that everyone was keeping up on those readings. Each student presented the results of research on their text, having read various scholarly discussions on it. There was a final exam.

But before those familiar elements took place, we began with orality. Everyone began a process of learning a story with me as a guide.

5. Whitney Shiner, *Proclaiming the Gospel: First-Century Performance of Mark* (Harrisburg, PA: Trinity, 2003) 11.

6. Joanna Dewey has reconstructed the oral nature and function of Mark based on textual evidence within Mark. See her fine article, "The Survival of Mark's Gospel: A Good Story?" *Journal of Biblical Literature* 123 (2004) 495–507.

7. Throughout the rest of this chapter, students' comments from unpublished classroom reflections will be cited with the student's name in the body of the text.

8. Elizabeth Struthers Malbon, *Hearing Mark: A Listener's Guide* (Harrisburg, PA: Trinity, 2002).

9. Doug Lipman, *Improving Your Storytelling* (Little Rock, AR: August House, 1999).

10. Boomershine, *Story Journey*.

Recognizing that storytellers in the ancient world learned the text through hearing it proclaimed out loud, we tried to simulate that process. I had already learned our first story by heart. I had chosen an important moment toward the end of the narrative when Jesus is dying and cries out from the cross to the God he can no longer see. Using a method I had learned from Tom Boomershine, I first asked them to watch as I told the story, complete with gestures and varied intonation. Then I invited them to comment on what they saw. After a brief conversation, it was their turn. I told them to repeat back to me the story as I told it. I would recite a short phrase and they would respond with the same words, gestures, and tones. We repeated this multiple times; with each repetition I lengthened the phrase. Every so often we would pause to look at the words and phrases that were repeated noting how they are put together in such a way as to help us recall the tale later. Finally, the students received a printed copy of the text. Even then each storyteller was not to look at the printed copy when she told the story; rather the text was for the partner to help the storyteller if she got stuck. Working in pairs, each tried to tell his partner the story while the listener followed along with the printed text. If the storyteller lost his train of thought, then his partner would cue him with the next gesture rather than a word. When the first storyteller had given it his best shot, they would switch roles. Most were surprised at how well they knew the text after only a half an hour of work. This is because the whole body, not only the eyes and the mind, were involved in this process.

The following week all fifteen students presented the same story, but we quickly learned that it was not exactly the same story every time. In fact, it was not the same story even twice. Each performance was unique, just as each performance of this story in the early church was also unique. The basic plot remained the same, but the emotional seasoning, pace, emphasis, and tonal qualities varied from teller to teller. Different perspectives also emerged as a result of gender, ethnicity, body type, or personal style. In the act of hearing multiple performances, we discovered that the story could not be reduced to a simple moral but was complex and capable of moving authentically in diverse directions. In the mouth of one, "My God! My God! Why did you abandon me?" (15:34) sounded like Jesus was asking, "Why *me* of all people?" In the voice of another the act of abandoning gained emphasis. Some screamed out to the heavens. Others muttered as they looked about in confusion. The different interpretations did not compete with each other but served to enrich the class's understanding of the text. As Amanda Schnelle pointed out, watching other interpretations tended to "add layers to my current understanding." This may have been one of the most important moments of the semester, as each person realized she could reach out to her audience in multiple valid ways through the same story.

Following the steps outlined by Boomershine, we next shared experiences from our own lives when we had felt abandoned, describing how Jesus' cry of abandonment connected with us personally. The students spoke of betrayal by friends, the deaths of relatives, and times of intense confusion. This personal connection strengthened the students' relationship with the story, drawing the story more profoundly into their hearts and giving their performance weight. They would carry Jesus' cry with them throughout the semester as they embraced other texts from Mark's gospel, and as they faced the inherent challenges of life.

During the remainder of the course, each student learned four selections from the gospel to tell to the class as story, received feedback, and shared with the class their discoveries from their research into and learning of the story. Knowing that they had to perform the text made the students personally interested in understanding the dynamics of a text; they would have to interpret each and every word in their performance. In the process of telling the story, the students learned new things about the text by experiencing the response of the audience. Watching others perform opened them up to new directions in their understanding of their own texts. Amanda's discussion of defilement helped Wes think about issues of uncleanliness in his text. Andrew's discussion of the temple authorities helped Jessica's understanding of the trial dynamics in her story.

Much of the work we did involved locating overlapping themes, language, and gestures in each other's stories. We created a set of common gestures we would use for people falling before Jesus, for casting out demons, for preaching, for healing, and for crossing over to the other side. We tried to build on the portrayals of characters that others had offered so that the story would be heard as a unified whole.

Over the course of the semester, a dynamic community was created in the classroom. Our learning was academically based but also playful. We respected each other but also challenged each other. More importantly, we enjoyed each other. We laughed often. We took turns being vulnerable in our storytelling but also took on authority when teaching about our texts. People regularly left more energized than they were when the period started. They depended on each other and worried less about grades than about the quality of our communal project. The students often brought a friend along to class because they wanted to share the experience they were having with others. Boomershine understood what he was talking about when he said, "Storytelling creates community. Persons who tell each other stories become friends. And men and women who know the same stories are bound together in special ways."[11]

Real learning took place over this semester. In addition to learning about the text and the ancient world, students sometimes found that their assumptions and presuppositions were shaken. Some of those who had studied the Bible all their lives learned how far they still had to go. Kiesha Priem spoke for many when she said, "I knew a lot less than I thought I did" about the dynamics of the biblical stories. Others who had not read the Bible at all found a story that they will carry with them into their future, a story worthy of engaging. The most consistent and radical transformation was the students' understanding of the identity of Jesus. Many of them had taken classes that discussed the humanity of Jesus in Mark's portrayal, but they did not really understand what this meant until they played Jesus themselves in flesh and blood. Wes Cain describes his discovery in this regard:

> I am so used to thinking of a Savior that walks on water, heals the sick, and raises others . . . from the dead that I never once thought about a Jesus that gets agitated at people's density and even angry at times. Jesus for me has always been the poster child for good behavior and someone who never crosses the line. This is not the Jesus seen in Mark's Gospel, though. Mark portrays a very human, very passionate Jesus that encourages people to see beyond their boundaries and themselves and not allow themselves to be limited to traditions and customs.

What is fascinating to me about Wes's comments is that through inhabiting Jesus in performance, he experienced the humanity of Jesus. The humanity of Jesus that he experienced challenged the traditions and customs of the first century world; but even more importantly Jesus showed up to challenge the traditions and customs of our own day. This became "good news" for many of them. Jonathan Lys states why this was so for him, "Grief, abandonment, shame, despair, and fear are much easier to bear

---

11. Ibid., 18.

when we realize that our savior experienced these same feelings." Those of us in the class discovered for ourselves what Boomershine promised us about the risen Christ in the first chapter of his book,

> Through the stories, Jesus Christ becomes present. There is a sense in which Jesus tells his own story, first to and through the evangelists and then to and through us. And when these moments of authentic connection take place, Jesus is really there. Thus, telling the stories of the Gospels is one of the forms of the real presence of Christ.[12]

The Word Heard

How is hearing the word performed to an audience different than reading a text to oneself? The reading of a text, of course, can be an engaging experience. One can get caught up in the story. Yet every year I have over one hundred students read Mark's gospel for my classes and rarely would they describe that primary reading experience as engaging. Even the students interested enough to take this whole course on Mark reported getting "lost in trudging through it" (Chris Crowder) when I required them to read it all in one sitting. Jessica Adame honestly reflected on her attempt to read through the gospel at the beginning of the course, "While reading it at home I was usually lying down in my bed before I fell asleep. The story was SO LONG that I didn't see the importance of the parables, riddles, and stories of abandonment. Instead I found myself speed reading through stories that seemed pretty similar." With the uniform fonts of the printed page she had an untextured experience of the story. She had difficulty knowing what she should be noticing or why things that were reported mattered. For others, their familiarity with the story was a barrier to a fresh hearing. As Jessica Matlack points out, "When I only read this story, my preconceived notions . . . override what I am reading."

In the presence of a prepared storyteller the audience experiences the texture of the story in all its newness. Through tone, gestures, emphasis, and pace the storytellers who had spent a semester learning about the whole story could draw the audience's attention to what matters within it. They could move the story off of the two-dimensional surface of the page and into the multiple dimensions of life. The audience received

12. Ibid., 21.

visual clues that guided them into the story world. The performers invoked a story world for the audience to enter and became the wise tour guides who know their way around the terrain well and could point out things that the audience might miss on its own.

When reading a text to oneself, the pace and tone of an episode is often something that you only sense after you have read it; normally we simply note that and do not go back to sound it properly in our heads. In performance, pace, tone, and gesture alerts the audience to what matters in a text. Often when beginning storytellers first learn a story, they are so concerned with words that they are not ready to guide anyone through the territory of the story world. They may speak of Jesus walking on water in the same tone one would use to describe crossing a street. They also might announce that Jesus fed thousands of people as though this is nothing unusual. But once they have moved beyond words into the texture of the story, they cue the audience to see what is astonishing. Suddenly each of the words in "walking on the sea" or "five thousand people" no longer are sounded as quarter notes like the other words in the sentence; each of these words becomes a whole note and the voice of the storyteller rises to an excited pitch, accompanied by emphatic gestures. The miracle is not lightly passed over as it might be in the untextured reading. The audience finds itself astonished and among those in the crowd present in the story.

Gestures are another tool that the storytellers use to help the audience make connections with the story. For example, a reader who has no memory of the stories of Israel might easily miss clues within the text that connect to those memories. For example, John the baptizer is described "wearing camel's hair with a leather band around his waist, and he was eating grasshoppers and wild honey" (1:6). An informed person might hear in this language an echo of prophet images like those from 2 Kgs 1:8 where the prophet Elijah is described or from Zech 13:4 where such language describes prophets in general. The storyteller, however, can help the less informed audience member to see this connection easily. John comes onto the scene right after the prophet Isaiah was invoked. The storyteller says, "As it is written in *Isaiah the prophet*," (1:2a) and he strikes a dramatic prophetic pose to accompany the introduction of Isaiah. Perhaps he raises his hand above his head with the index finger extended. Then he holds that gesture as he begins to speak Isaiah's prophetic word, "Look, I am sending my messenger ahead of you, who will pave your way, the voice of one shouting in the desert, 'Prepare the way of the Lord, make his paths direct.'" (1:2b–3) The act of prophetic speech is tethered to a particular gesture. Then immediately after this, John shows up "in the desert, proclaiming" (1:4) and the storyteller, now acting as the character John, makes the same prophetic gesture. By the time the descriptions of John's clothing and diet are offered, the audience already understands John both as the one prophesied by Isaiah and as a prophet himself. This prophetic gesture would be used later when John prophetically challenges Herod or when Jesus mentions John's ministry. Likewise prophetic dimensions of Jesus' proclamation of the kingdom of God are made clearer by association with this gesture. Each time Jesus "proclaims" the storyteller strikes this gesture for a moment. When others report that some say Jesus is John raised from the dead, or Elijah, or one of the other prophets this gesture reinforces the prophetic dimensions in the story. Finally, when Jesus disrupts the sellers and moneychangers in the temple, the pose reappears, helping the audience to understand the prophetic dimension of this event. None of this need be done mechanically; the storyteller subtly guides the hearer into the story's territory, showing the common paths that crisscross it. Although I have emphasized how this storytelling dynamic helps initiate the uninformed person, the same dynamic also provides the informed person with a more holistic experience of the whole story.

Gestures like these help connect story elements but they also allow the audience to see what is left unsaid. This is especially true of certain patterns of repetition in the Gospel. In the beginning of the Gospel, one of the storytellers, Andew Dietzel, enacted the call of the fishing disciples. In the first of the stories while playing the role of Jesus, he made a beckoning gesture as he said, "Come after me, and I'll make you become fishers for people" (1:17). Moments later he showed Jesus calling another set of brothers with the same gesture. In this second call story, we are not told what Jesus says but only that he calls them. Yet the repetition of the beckoning gesture helps the audience remember the content of the first call, and transfer that to the second.

Another helpful technique is showing the dynamics of interaction between characters. The following passage is difficult for a silent reader of the text to understand even at a basic level. Jesus says to the Pharisees and legal experts:

How well you nullify the ordinance of God in order to establish your tradition! For Moses said, "Honor your father and your mother," and "Whoever pronounces misfortune on father or mother must surely die." But *you* say, "If a man says to his father or mother, 'Whatever might have been a benefit to you from me is *corban*'"—that is, devoted to God—you no longer allow him to do anything at all for his father or mother, thus annulling the word of God by your tradition that you handed on. (7:9–12)

So what is going on? Let me walk you through how our storyteller told this same story.

> [*She picks a few people in the front row who become for her the Pharisees and legal experts. Striking our prophetic pose she looks them in the eyes.*] How well you nullify the ordinance of God in order to establish your tradition! For Moses said, "Honor your father [*she points to a man to the right of the legal experts*] and your mother [*pointing also the woman next to the father*]," and [*still speaking to the Pharisees and legal experts*] "Whoever pronounces misfortune on father [*gestures toward the person chosen as 'father'*] or mother [*also toward the 'mother'*] must surely die." But *you* say, [*invoking the prophetic gesture*] "If a man [*Jessica indicates that she will now be the man to which she refers*] says to his father or mother, [*she speaks to the parents*] 'Whatever might have been a benefit to you [*she makes a gesture as though she is about to hand them some money*] from me is *corban* [*she quickly pulls back the invisible gift she had been offering them*]'"—that is, devoted to God [*putting skeptical quotation marks around the last word with her voice, she takes the would-be gift away from the parents and sets it in the legal expert's lap*]—you no longer allow him to do anything at all for his father or mother [*she looks the Pharisees and legal experts in the eyes, indicating with a head nod toward the parents*], thus annulling the word of God [*prophetic gesture*] by your tradition that you handed on [*shaking her head*].

In this telling, the complicated dynamics of the conflict become clear. The legal experts are using their tradition to take money from families in need in order to fill their own treasury. They are using God's name to justify their shady dealings. Jessica has helped the audience literally to see what is going on. When this theme returns again a few chapters later in terms of the exploitation of widows by the legal experts, gestures are used again to help the audience make that connection as well. When hearing this story portrayed, many audience members experience anger at the institutional injustice of this tradition and the cost it has on the vulnerable. Emotional content is communicated as a central aspect of the story. Jonathan Lys summarizes this well, saying, "Storytellings bring in human thoughts and feelings, which elicit the same in the audience." This emotional content means that one experiences a good performance with the whole self.

Perhaps the most surprising and jarring thing for many people upon hearing the gospel performed for the first time is how often they find themselves laughing. Biblical scholar Donald Juel confessed, "I did not recall ever laughing to myself when reading through Mark."[13] But he also notes that the performance of Mark's gospel that he has witnessed stimulated laughter. For example, Jesus tells a funny parable of the kingdom of God being like a weed.

When a person reads the Gospel silently, it often feels like a series of semi-related fragments. When the story is heard in performance, it feels whole. While it is possible to engage the whole Gospel of Mark in one sitting through reading it, very few people do this and even experienced readers may feel that the narrative jumps randomly from section to section. Donald Juel noted how different his experience of those difficult transitions were in performance:

> The person who "performed" Mark . . . recited in such a way that the breaks in the story were not a problem. The sense of coherence was accomplished in several ways, like changing positions and looking at different sections of the audience. It worked. The audience has little sense that the Gospel was deficient as a narrative. There were gaps and jumps, but the way they were handled by the performer made them enticing rather than irritating and distracting.[14]

We have seen how clarity can be achieved and connections made through storytelling practices; we also have begun to show how something greater is going on than simply understanding what is happening. As David Rhoads writes:

> The audience participates in more ways than understanding. Words and stories do not just have denotations of meaning. They also have an impact on people. We are not dealing simply with the notion of conveying information about events to an audience. The narrative is not a vehicle for an idea, as if we could get the idea or

13. Donald Juel, "The Strange Silence of the Bible," *Interpretation* 51 (1997) 8.
14. Ibid.

the theology and then no longer need the story. Nor is the story an example to illustrate an idea. The story itself has energy and power. The story affects the whole person—heart, soul, mind, and body.[15]

The storytelling does this by drawing in the audience so that they become participants in the story world. They become parents or legal experts or any other number of characters within the story. Jessica Matlack states, "I feel like I am part of the story. Sometimes, one of the storytellers will come right up to me and direct a statement or an accusation directly at me. In these instances, I not only feel like I am seeing the story played out in person; I feel as if I am part of the story, whether I am doing something to help the Lord or that will result in his death."

This is perhaps the biggest gift that performance offers. The audience enters the story with their whole being. Not only do their minds get addressed, their bodies and spirits are engaged. When audience members later speak of their experience, they report things like, "When I heard *Jesus* cry out from the cross . . ." not "Ryan, when *you said* that Jesus cried out from the cross." Boomershine calls this "the rhetoric of implication" and claims that it is fundamental to the gospel stories but is only experienced through performance.[16] The power of this experience is expressed by Jessica Adame, who spoke of the tensions between grief and hope she herself experienced as the father of the possessed boy cried out, "I trust, help my lack of trust!" (9:24)

Conclusion

The experience of hearing the gospel proclaimed is very different than that of reading it to oneself. One of my students, Brad Eubanks, with the exaggeration characteristic of a recent convert claimed that the written text of Mark is related to the original performance of Mark's Gospel in the way that paper is related to the living tree from which it was made. He went on to say that the Word of God should not be experienced as something that "once lived [but that now] has had the life mechanically

15. David Rhoads, *Reading Mark, Engaging the Gospel* (Minneapolis: Fortress, 2004) 185.

16. Thomas E. Boomershine, "Biblical Storytelling and Biblical Scholarship," paper presented at the Network of Biblical Storytellers Scholars Seminar, August 2004. Online: <http://www.nobsseminar.org/exegesis.html#boomershine>.

sucked out of it." In the performance of the gospel, the word comes alive. Its impact is profound, direct, and immediate. This impact is holistic. The whole story speaks to the each person with their heart, soul, mind, and body as well as to the whole community that has gathered. The performance gathers together our bodies, our emotions, and our lived experiences carrying them for a moment in the story of Jesus. The whole of our lives find dwelling places in the spaciousness created by the story. As William Ryan Brown concludes, "events in our lives are empowered and given meaning by being connected with God's story."

Questions

1. What preparation for performance proved essential to the students in the course?

2. What key difference do you notice between the description of the performance of Mark and your own practices of reading the gospel?

3. Given that storytelling has such a powerful effect, what ethical issues do you think the storyteller needs to consider in order to avoid manipulating the audience?

8

LIFE, STORY, AND THE BIBLE

Marti J. Steussy

Introduction

PEOPLE TELL STORIES. PEOPLE HAVE TOLD STORIES IN EVERY
known culture. We are fascinated by stories long before we learn—in-
dividually or societally—to manipulate abstract ideas or ask penetrating
questions about the relation of story to fact. Indeed, story's importance
to children and less technologically complex cultures sometimes leads
us to describe story as a "primitive" phenomenon. But adults in modern
Western culture remain vitally interested in story, as we can see from the
money we spend on movies and television and the gigabytes of stories and
jokes we forward to one another on the Internet. If story is "primitive," it
is so in the sense of primal appeal, not in the sense of being something
that we advance beyond.

Contemporary studies in neurobiology and psychology suggest story
is not only common among humans, but *necessary*: the left brain's com-
pulsion to create a coherent story out of events is so strong that when
it does not have access to a plausible story it will fabricate one, which it
does not recognize as fictional.[1] The brain's eagerness to produce a story
consistent with past experience and stories we have heard as well as what
has actually happened can even lead us to revise our own autobiographical

---

1. See Michael S. Gazzaniga, *The Mind's Past* (Berkeley: University of California
Press, 1998).

memories.[2] So not only are we are story-makers, but stories make *us*: we will reshape our very memories and concepts of self to fit them to the stories we hear. When the process leads to unreliable testimony, it creates real problems. Most of the time, though, story's power functions helpfully, allowing us to learn from other people's experiences and not just our own. What we learn from stories merges with our own memories, themselves sculpted "for narrative purposes with a view toward meaning and signification, not toward the end of somehow 'preserving' the facts themselves," into the map of the universe by which we make both momentous and everyday decisions.[3]

Let's pause here to consider what stories are made of (plot, characters, world, tone),[4] with a few comments on special dynamics that arise around these aspects in biblical stories, then come back to the question of story's impact on our lives.

Plot

What *is* a story? Sheer description of a scene doesn't make a story: something has to *happen*. Stories have, as Aristotle said of tragedy, a "beginning, middle, and end"—a plot.[5] We assume that story events are connected in some meaningful way, most often by direct causation (although other types of linkage also occur, as when similar or contrasting events are juxtaposed). Thus, in Mark 5:21–43, we get the healing of the woman with the flow of blood, embedded in the account of Jesus' healing of Jairus' daughter. From one standpoint, the healing of the woman interrupts the story of the healing of the daughter, but from another it underscores the role of having faith/believing. If the relation of parts in a plot is not obvious,

2. For a readable overview of the vast literature on induced and altered memory, see Daniel L. Schachter, *The Seven Sins of Memory: How the Mind Forgets and Remembers* (Boston: Houghton Mifflin, 2001) 112–37.

3. J. Bruner and C. Feldman, "Group Narrative as a Cultural Context of Autobiography," in *Remembering Our Past: Studies in Autobiographical Memory*, ed. D. C. Rubin (London: Cambridge University Press, 1996) 293.

4. I draw this set of categories from Wesley Kort, whose 1988 book *Story, Text, and Scripture* (University Park: Penn State University Press, 1988) has been formative in my thinking about the nature and implications of Scripture's story form. Kort uses the term "atmosphere" for what I call "world."

5. Aristotle *Poetics* 7–9.

we will struggle to find it; if we can't, we generally feel as if the story is defective, or that the storyteller has let us down.

The importance of plot in story is surely related to our need to understand causality and repeating patterns in real life. Our very survival depends on our ability to perceive the connections between events: I have a terrible stomachache, is it because I ate those berries for lunch? In real life, however, causal connections are obscured by red herrings and sheer "noise": should I associate the stomachache with the berries for lunch, being rude to Uncle Joe, kissing cousin Susie who had a sniffly nose, eating funny-smelling meat at breakfast, or stepping on an unusually colored cricket? In a story, by contrast, we expect to be able to perceive patterns more clearly, to practice meaning-finding with a higher chance of success. In this sense, stories may present us with what evolutionary biologists call a "supernormal stimulus"—something similar to what would be important in real life, but more pronounced (as lipstick produces an even more pronounced version of the flushed lips of a romantically interested partner). Some stories, including most biblical stories, are very spare in what they tell us. Others, such as Marilynne Robinson's novel *Gilead*, cover a broad range of events and offer much descriptive detail. Robinson's details are not, however, superfluous—they have overtones and allusions inside and outside the novel that add to the richness of meaning. The meaningfulness of each detail is part of why we might describe both the spare biblical stories and the lush novel as well-crafted.

Another trait shared by almost all story plots is that there's a problem: a conflict, tension, or lack. It may be a very obvious problem, like needing food in a time of famine (Gen 12:10–20). It may be a very subtle one, like feeling that one's accomplishments aren't satisfying. The Gospel of Luke, like many stories in the First Testament, begins with a report of childlessness. But King Herod's name in 1:5 reminds the hearer of a larger problem—God's seeming abandonment of God's people to oppression—and by the time a first-century audience heard the Magnificat (Luke 1:47–55), they would already be suspecting that Elizabeth's old-age pregnancy and Mary's virgin one might be moves toward God's solving of that larger issue.

While the Bible's overall view of history is usually characterized as having a happy ending, we should notice that problems in individual biblical stories are not always resolved. Abram is to father a multitude of nations and inherit all the land of Canaan (Gen 17:4–8), but at the end of

Genesis his descendants (at least in the chosen line of Jacob) live in Egypt and possess only a burial cave in Canaan. Moses is said to have spoken to God "face to face, as one speaks to a friend" (Exod 33:11; see also Num 12:8),[6] but he dies without being able to enter the land to which he has spent his life bringing an often-ungrateful people, and no one will visit his grave, because its location is unknown. Early copies of the Gospel of Mark end with the words, "they said nothing to anyone, for they were afraid" (16:8). What are we to make of this? It should at the very least remind us that the Jewish and Christian storytellers of the Bible knew what it is like to live in a history that does not arrive at resolution in the short term.

Character

Another highly visible element of story is characters. Literary theorists often distinguish between "round" characters, who are complex individuals that show growth in the course of a story, and "flat characters," whose identities are defined by a few key traits and either don't change or do so in very predictable stereotyped ways. We find both types in the Bible.

Contemporary Bible readers typically have plenty of questions about biblical characters and their motives. Sometimes the problem is that we aren't familiar with the culture of the ancient world. "Why does Naomi tell Ruth and Orpah to return to their families?" Well, *she* says it's because she isn't likely to conceive additional sons for them to marry (thus referring to the custom that the dead husband's brother should impregnate a childless widow, Deut 25:5–6), but most people want more explanation (we will return shortly to the idea that a biblical character's words don't always give us truth or the whole truth). What modern readers often don't know, but ancient audiences would have known, is that Moabites, especially Moabite women, didn't have too good a reputation in Israel.[7] Naomi's reluctance to have the widows return with her, her failure to introduce Ruth to the women of Bethlehem, and her silence when they lay Ruth's baby in her arms at the end of the story may all have to do with ancient ethnic prejudice to which modern readers are blind.

---

6. Bible citations are from the NRSV unless otherwise indicated.

7. Danna Nolan Fewell and David M. Gunn, "'A Son Is Born To Naomi!': Literary Allusions and Interpretation in the Book of Ruth," *Journal for the Study of the Old Testament* 13 (1988) 99–108.

At other times, our confusion about biblical characters has to do with our expectation that they will be good role models. "Why does Abraham lie about Sarah being his sister?" (Gen 12:10–20; 20). This is an interesting question because it shouldn't need to be asked at all. The stories very straightforwardly tell us Abraham's motive: he is afraid the foreigners will kill him in order to take his beautiful wife (12:11–12; 20:11) although we only know that Abraham fears this, not that his fears are realistic: in both stories the foreigners actually act quite honorably towards Abraham.[8] But many Bible readers *expect* Abraham to be a truth-teller, so the incident bothers them.

The fact that Bible characters can lie means we ought to be a little more careful than we usually are about taking everything characters say as "gospel truth." I have, for instance, more than once heard 1 Sam 15:29 ("the Glory of Israel . . . is not a mortal, that he should change his mind") quoted as proof that God can never repent. But according to that very chapter of 1 Samuel, the prophet Samuel is mistaken in saying that God never changes his mind (the Hebrew word here is *niham*), because earlier in the chapter (15:11) God has announced, "I regret [translated differently, but the same word, *niham*] that I made Saul king," and the chapter closes with the storyteller's comment that "the Lord was sorry [the same word, *niham*] that he had made Saul king over Israel" (15:35). Since we are told twice in this very chapter that God has repented/has changed his mind/is sorry (*niham*), Samuel's implication that only mortals *niham*, and never God, cannot be taken as an absolute truth.

To return to the subject of why we are sometimes confused by Bible characters, let's take another question: why does Abraham lie about Sarah *twice*? Old Testament scholars often answer that we are looking at two versions of a single legend. The storyteller (often referred to as "J") in Gen 12 doesn't seem too worried about Abraham's lie, while the storyteller in Gen 20 (often referred to as "E") attempts to exonerate Abraham by telling us that Sarah really was his half-sister (20:12), although this doesn't erase Abraham's deceit with regard to her being his wife. As if this weren't enough, in Gen 26 Abraham's son Isaac tells the same lie ("she is my sister") to the same king! While in some cases receiving them as irrec-

---

8. Randall C. Bailey, "They're Nothing but Incestuous Bastards: The Polemical Use of Sex and Sexuality in Hebrew Canon Narratives," in *Reading from This Place*, vol. 1: *Social Location and Biblical Interpretation in the United States,* ed. Fernando Segovia and Mary Ann Tolbert (Minneapolis : Fortress, 1995) 121–38.

oncilable alternatives does seem the best way to make sense of duplicated or contradictory stories,[9] in many other cases the tension contributes to our picture of the characters. Whether or not the various wife/sister stories come from different sources, having them in sequence gives us an Abraham who, like the rest of us, doesn't learn too well from his mistakes, and whose family exhibits the all-too-familiar tendency for children to repeat the mistakes of their parents.

Finally, and not least, we may be puzzled by biblical characters because we are supposed to be. "God has brought them out of Egypt, given them water, given them food, why do they still murmur?" Good question. It's probably exactly what the storyteller wants the audience to ask, followed by, "Well, if we think they should have been able to trust God, shouldn't we be able to also?" Why can't the sons of Zebedee understand that Jesus' kingdom isn't about position and power? (Mark 10:35–35). Well, have we quit jockeying for position *yet?* Why can't David see that he needs to discipline his children? Because God's plans play out in odd ways. As Robert Alter has famously said, "there is a deep and abiding mystery in character as conceived by the biblical writers."[10] Bible characters can be puzzling because, like the people we know (and are) ourselves, they are complex.

Our confusion about the Bible's human characters may then rise from several causes: not understanding the ancient culture, being frustrated in our expectation that the characters will act as "role models," the fact that the Bible seems to have been composed over a considerable period of time by people living in various places and with different points of view, and the sheer realism of biblical storytelling. However, we should not depart from the topic of confusion about biblical characters without pointing out that *God* is a character, too.

God, like any other biblical character, becomes known to us in the Bible's stories via what the storytellers choose to tell us. Of course, most of us aren't reading the Bible for the first time, and even if we are we have probably already formed some opinions about God (even those who vigorously deny belief in God typically have a quite firm idea of whom it is they don't believe in). Not uncommonly, these well-formed ideas

9. For example, I find "alternative version" the best way to account for the differences between 1 Sam 16:14–23 and 17:55–58 on how Saul meets David; or 1 Sam 17:49–51 and 2 Sam 21:19 on who killed Goliath.

10. Robert Alter, *The Art of Biblical Narrative* (New York: Basic, 1981) 126.

influence our hearing of the stories so profoundly that we may not even notice when the characterization of God departs from what we already "know." For instance, Gen 11:5 says, "The Lord *came down to see* the city and the tower, which mortals had built" (emphasis added). This sits awkwardly with our usual idea that God is everywhere and can see everything, but the idea that this storyteller has a more limited view of God—and perhaps a more exalted conception of human powers—than most modern Bible readers is reinforced one verse later (v. 6) when God proposes confusing the people's speech because otherwise "nothing that they propose to do now will be impossible for them."

The fact that God is a character often comes into clearest focus for us when we begin comparing different biblical materials. Second Samuel 24's story of David purchasing the threshing floor on which the temple was eventually built begins with a statement that "the anger of the LORD was kindled against Israel, and he incited David against them, saying, 'Go, count the people of Israel and Judah.'" The version of the story in 1 Chr 21 begins, "Satan [or, "an adversary," which is what the word *satan* means in Hebrew] stood up against Israel, and incited David to count the people of Israel." The 2 Samuel version, in which God then punishes David (or rather, David's people) for what God has incited David to do, leaves a rather different impression of God than does 1 Chronicles, in which God punishes David for an act incited by someone else! Churchly language about the Bible as the Word of God may lead us to expect a single and straightforward report about God's character, but the varied biblical stories characterize God in differing and sometimes conflicting ways.

World

Plot and characters are not the only components of storytelling, although they tend to be the ones we notice most quickly. Another important, although often unconsidered, aspect of story is what science fiction writers call the "story world" or "story universe": the framework of what is possible and probable in the world the story's characters inhabit.

One tends to notice a biblical story world most when it differs in some explicit way from the world one normally inhabits (or, more precisely, from the world one believes that one inhabits). So, for instance, the gospel's world includes demons, powerful malevolent spirits that ruin the lives of those they possess unless driven away by persons with sufficient spiritual authority. How are such stories to be understood by modern audiences? For those modern audience members who believe that they *have* encountered demons, there may be no particular problem. For those less convinced of the reality of demons, their presence in New Testament stories may suggest that possession could happen in our world as well. Others suppose that demons were real "then" but not "now," that the biblical world was materially different than our own.

Still others, noting that the symptoms of demon possession resemble epileptic seizures, may retell the demon-banishing stories to themselves as ones about the healing of epilepsy. Such naturalistic explanations are popular both among those uncomfortable with the concept of "miracle" and those who want science's authority to buttress the Bible's claims. But such attempts to understand story events in terms of our own worldview get in the way of understanding what ancient storytellers wanted us to hear. For instance, it has been proposed that the reason Elijah's altar on Mount Carmel caught fire so easily was that Elijah's agents had poured not water (1 Kgs 18:33–35) but naphtha (a flammable hydrocarbon, like lighter fluid) around the altar. But such a naturalizing explanation shifts the story's focus from a contest between alleged gods (Baal and the Lord) to Elijah's own cleverness. It completely reverses the point of the water pouring, which is to underscore the extraordinariness of the altar's combustion, not to bring it into the realm of normalcy. To understand the point of the story, we have to let the water be water, even though it may raise a problem in connecting the story's world with our own.

While it is relatively easy to notice the aspects of story worldview which are explicitly mentioned, it can be trickier to notice what isn't mentioned. One thing that receives very little mention is egalitarian relationships: both Testaments depict worlds in which social relationships, even between brothers or sisters, always have "up" and "down" status directions (an older brother normally has social precedence over the younger). This means that listening to Bible stories will give us lots of examples of how people relate when one owes deference to another, but they do little to show us how things might operate under the ideal of equal dignity for every human being. They show us how families operate in a system where marriage is arranged by parents and in which intimacy needs are often fulfilled in relationships other than the marriage, but not much about the dynamics of marriages chosen by partners on the basis of a love relationship. Indeed, most of what we see about marriage in the Bible comes in the course of stories about court life (the world of the rich and famous) or the lives of the patriarchs (individuals whose relationships symbolize the relationships of the later peoples and tribes descended from them), so from the Bible itself we don't know all that much about what ordinary marriages or family life were like.

What goes unsaid in a story world can be confusing when later audiences with different assumptions hear the stories. New Testament storytellers could assume that their audiences knew of the Pharisees as a particularly devoted set of religious teachers who put enormous energy into trying to practice what they preached and live faithfully in every detail of life. With this assumption in place, there would be an enormous shock value to stories in which Jesus accuses the Pharisees of having their values in the wrong place. The stories have a quite different effect on modern audiences for whom the term "pharisaic" has come to mean "hypocritically self-righteous." We assume that what Pharisees say will be wrong-headed and wrong-hearted, so we experience the stories quite differently than did ancient audiences who admired the Pharisees and expected consistency and insight from them!

While in many ways the worlds of biblical stories reflect the conditions and assumptions of the "real worlds" in which their tellers lived, a story world may also differ from the normal one in ways governed by the rules of a particular story type (genre). A story that begins "once upon a time" signals us to hear with ears appropriate to a fairy tale; we know that our central character is likely to be a stepchild, quite possibly the youngest of three or seven same-sex sibs, and will probably receive unexpected help from a fairy godmother or talking animal. We are quite capable of enjoying and finding meaning in such stories even though most of us don't believe in fairies or talking animals. We also enjoy chase scenes in which multiple vehicles collide, flip over, and explode without killing the major chase participants, though such events would be highly unlikely in our actual world. Clearly we make important differentiations between reality and story conventions. At the same time, our differentiations are not as absolute as we might like to think. Studies show, for instance, that watching crime shows on television increases people's sense that they are likely to be victims of crime in real life.[11] The ways in which our brains relate "story" to "reality" are complex!

We normally register genre signals and adjust our story reception accordingly without even realizing we're doing it. Misreading the genre cues can substantially distort our experience of a story.[12] For instance, trying to understand the book of Job on the assumption that it gives us a literal account of historical events is even more difficult than reading it as an example of the ancient genre of "disputation" in which different points of view are juxtaposed as a form of philosophical debate. With the Bible, genre assessment is complicated by the fact that for most readers today, "Bible" is itself a genre, carrying certain implications about seriousness, accuracy, and religious intent which may in some cases be quite different from the genre assumptions of the persons who put particular biblical stories into writing (for instance, some fairly large stretches of First Testament narrative may have been composed to provide a sense of national identity or support a particular political leader rather than teach religion). In such cases, do we try to hear the story in terms of its "original" genre, or does the intervening tradition authorize us to look for something the original tellers may not have intended?

Tone

World involves what can happen in a story. Tone has to do with the teller's attitude towards various aspects of that world. Judgment may sometimes be explicitly stated, as when the narrator says in 1 Kgs 13:33, "Jeroboam did not turn from his evil way"; but is often expressed more subtly by genre, the nuances of word choice, and patterns of allusion. So, for instance, the heavy repetition and exaggerated scale of descriptions in the Hebrew book of Esther give the story the slapstick tone of parody. The reported killing of seventy-five thousand in 9:16 is somewhat less disturbing in this cartoonish world than it would be in a realistically narrated one.

---

11. Kenneth Dowler, "Media Consumption and Public Attitudes toward Crime and Justice: The Relationship between Fear of Crime, Punitive Attitudes, and Perceived Police Effectiveness," *Journal of Criminal Justice and Popular Culture* 10 (2003) 109–26. Online: http://Albany.edu/scj/jcjpc/vol10is2/dowler.pdf.

12. For an amusing example, see James Thurber's short story, "The MacBeth Murder Mystery," in *My World and Welcome to It* (New York: Harvest, 1969) 33–39. Online: http://userhome.brooklyn.cuny.edu/anthro/jbeatty/COURSES/Macbeth/thurber.htm.

When a story is told aloud, as biblical stories would have been in the ancient world, tone becomes a matter not only of the story's words but of the voice tone and expression of the teller. A storyteller who sets off the description of Ruth as a "Moabitess" by pausing and perhaps lifting an eyebrow will call attention to the ethnic dynamics in the story. The same teller, by adding a touch of impatience to Naomi's exhortations to the Moabite women to return to their homes (1:8–9 and 11–13), and an accent of peevishness to her "call me bitter" speech (1:20–21), while giving great authenticity to Bethlehemite attestations of Ruth's character (2:6–7, 11–2; 3:10–11, and 4:15) can clearly communicate that there is a problem with Naomi's attitudes towards the Moabitess. If the teller, however, gives Naomi's "go back" a tone of deep concern and does "call me bitter" with quiet resignation, the hearer is likely to experience the story as a sweet tale of family love and loyalty.

The example of Ruth tells us that the tone of a story is not simply determined by words on a page, but can be interpreted in different ways by tellers without varying the verbatim wording at all. Reception will also depend on the sensibilities of the audience, whose own background and experiences will influence what they notice about the telling and what meanings they assign. So, for instance, one student assumed that when Job's sons would "invite their three sisters to eat and drink with them" (1:4), the stage was being set for alcohol-lubricated sexual molestation, although most other readers see this as a report of good relationships in Job's wealthy, successful family. The ability of stories to support multiple valuative readings means that arguments over what a Bible story "teaches" may be irresolvable—or, perhaps, it means the stories "teach" something more complex than easily discernible precepts.

Life and Story

Earlier in this essay, I suggested that part of story's fascination for us is that it provides a super-normal stimulus, "more life-like than life." This means, however, that a story is not simply a reproduction of life as we experience it. Instead it is a crafted work of art that highlights some elements, downplays or completely omits others, and casts various evaluative lights upon them. We tend to treat stories, especially ones which concern historical events, as if they were windows onto what happened.

But even when every detail of a story is historically accurate, the story is no mere window. Instead, like a painting or film, it presents very select aspects from a particular angle in words that prompt us to arrive at particular evaluations or at least to ask some questions rather than others about the event.[13] Sometimes a storyteller shows us the action from an angle that will remind us of some other familiar scene, as when Luke reports Jesus' discussions about discipleship with James, John, and other would-be followers in terms that invite us to ponder the similarities and contrasts between Elijah and Jesus (compare Luke 9:54–62 with 1 Kgs 18:38, 19:11–21, and 2 Kgs 1:9–16). Or perhaps it invites us to attend to different elements than would normally attract our attention, as with the book of Ruth's positive attention to a Moabitess, or unsettles our usual expectations about how things will go, as when Jesus tells a Syro-Phoenician woman that casting a demon from her daughter is not a priority, then reverses his decision in the face of her response (Mark 7:24–30).

In some instances, biblical tellers use meaning-making strategies that actually interfere with the sense of looking through a window. In Dan 2:1, for example, the detail of a dream in the *second year* of Nebuchadnezzar's reign prompts us to think of the dream Pharaoh had "after two whole years" in Gen 41:4. The book of Daniel's editor apparently considered this allusion to Joseph's story more important than having a smooth timeline (the "second year" detail sits awkwardly with the fact that Nebuchadnezzar was in power for some years before he brought Jewish captives to Babylon, after which Daniel undergoes three years of training before entering Nebuchadnezzar's service). Matthew and Luke trace Jesus' ancestry to David *via Joseph,* even though the extraordinary circumstances of Jesus' conception might be thought to render Joseph's family tree irrelevant. Such use of symbolic details means that we need to ask not just about the events that happen (the kinds of questions we might ask about something we see through a window) but about why they are presented as they are (the kinds of questions prompted by a painting). But even these questions may not give us final answers about what the stories "mean."

---

13 The window/painting images come from Peter W. Macky, "The Coming Revolution: The New Literary Approach to the New Testament," in *A Guide to Contemporary Hermeneutics,* ed. Donald K. McKim (Grand Rapids: Eerdmans, 1986) 263–79; cited by Phyllis Trible in *Rhetorical Criticism: Context, Method, and the Book of Jonah,* Guides to Biblical Scholarship (Minneapolis: Fortress, 1994) 97.

What *do* stories mean? Most of us read novels and short stories and watch plays and movies without feeling any need to report their "lessons," but we treat Bible stories quite differently. Western culture prizes clearly stateable facts and ideas. Therefore we tend to assume, without even thinking about it, that what is most important about Scripture can and should be extracted as facts or ideas—the "lessons" of the Bible. Asked why the Bible uses story and poetry instead of presenting "lessons" straight up, most people will respond that story and poetry are "more interesting" or "easier to read." Such an analysis dismisses the story and poetry forms of the Bible as a pleasant but optional sugar coating that makes the "lessons" easier to swallow. It fails to ask whether the story and poetry forms might function in ways which *cannot be reduced* to "teachings."[14]

I suggest that the story form of Scripture (along with its poetry) indeed supports artistic forms of knowing that cannot be reduced to fixed statements or instructions. First, even in terms of stateable content each story contains much more (especially in the nuances of world and tone) than can be captured in the one-sentence "lessons" that we typically try to extract. Second, we react to stories (especially if we hear/see them told rather than simply reading them) with our whole selves, experiencing a range of physical and emotional reactions (muscles twitching in imagined acts with the characters, nervous systems recalling sounds, sights, smells, tastes, and feelings, memory making conscious and unconscious links with our own lives). A "lesson" approach gives us something we can manipulate in our very limited conscious mental workspace, and an answer for somebody who asks, "what did the story teach?" but the story itself touches the wide array of unconscious and subconscious processing mechanisms that feed into and largely control our conscious workspace.[15] In real life, what we learn from being consciously taught pales by comparison with all the things we learn unconsciously. Stories similarly affect us in the broad spaces where we *live*, not just the narrow place where we think.

I have already sketched some ways in which a teller's handling of character, plot, world, and tone may suggest particular views of reality even in genres which don't claim to be realistic depictions of life. It would

14. On our culture's preference for facts and ideas, and the non-reducibility of story to such, I am again following Kort.

15. On the limitations of conscious workspace and the large role played by preconscious processing, see Joseph LeDoux, *The Synaptic Self: How Our Brains Become Who We Are* (New York: Penguin, 2003); and Gazzinaga, *The Mind's Past*.

be a mistake, however, to suppose that a story's influence on us depends solely on factors in the story (or storytelling) itself. As we have also seen, different people or even the same person at different times may respond in different ways to the same story, depending on how we inhabit the room that the story gives for interpretation. Even relatively odd, seemingly off-the-wall responses, such as my student's suspicions about the partying of Job's children, can be important, as they allow us to process urgent issues of our own lives. Here is where thinking in terms of story dynamics may prompt a very different approach than the lesson-extraction strategy: the "lesson" approach usually seeks an objective teaching upon which different interpreters can be expected to agree, while a story dynamic approach is more comfortable with subjective, non-uniform responses (although it may still raise questions about the correspondence of interpretations to the material being interpreted). While a reader (or hearer)-response approach has more room for subjectivity, it need not be purely individualistic: the sharing of responses to story can be a highly effective and educational community-building process that stretches people's worldviews in a way that lesson-extraction does not.

Even preachers, who are generally quite determined to find the "lesson" in each story they encounter, regularly report that stories don't hold still: each time the preacher returns to a familiar story, she or he discovers something new in it. This is because our relationship to stories, like our relationship to our own memories, is a living one. We take up both stories and actual experience in an interactive meaning-making process that informs our schemata of perceiving, feeling, understanding, and acting.[16] Our making of stories and the stories' making of us together shape the experience of human life.

Questions

1. The author claims that as we make stories the stories make us. What are some of the key stories that have shaped who you are?

---

16. The discipline of narrative therapy centers around this process, for an introduction see the essays in Robyn Fivush and Catherine A. Haden, eds., *Autobiographical Memory and the Construction of A Narrative Self: Developmental and Cultural Perspectives* (Philadelphia: Erlbaum, 2003).

2. What do you notice when you analyze one of those personal stories in terms of plot, character, world, and tone?

3. Which of the observations in this chapter unsettled your assumptions about stories in the Bible? Why did you find them unsettling? Return to the biblical text of one of the stories discussed and locate the dynamics that the author cites. Do you see the evidence she cites from the text?

9

TAKING PLACE/TAKING UP SPACE

Richard W. Swanson

OVER THE MILLENNIA, AS JEWS AND CHRISTIANS HAVE READ and studied biblical texts, we have developed deeply detailed methods of study. We have studied the history of the text and the pre-history. We have studied the structure of the words and of the narrative. We have meditated upon the numerical value of the letters of individual words and upon the relationship between the Bible and the large complexes of texts that surround it in the ancient world. We have developed taxonomies of orthography that allow us to offer hypotheses about the nature of scribal practices in the ancient world.

All of these methods study biblical narrative as it lies pinned flat on a page. The interpretive gain from the centuries of text-based study, from yeshiva to university, is immense. None of us can imagine studying the Bible without having at least remembered recourse to text-critical studies, form-critical studies, source-critical studies, redaction-critical studies, literary-critical studies. All of these valuable and productive modes of engagement examine biblical narrative laid out on the pages of a book.

Yet none of these biblical narratives started its life as a page-text to be studied by silent readers, whether in a yeshiva or a university or a pious Bible study group. Even the most generous assessments of literacy rates in the ancient world conclude that the vast majority of the population (even among urban elites) could not read, and since neither Jewish nor Christian communities were populated primarily by cultural elites, the literacy rates in those communities would have been much lower. For these communities to have any awareness of biblical narrative, and for the narrative to have any real impact on them, some sort of live performance would have been necessary (see the chapters by Hearon and Shiner). And since private, silent reading is a relatively recent innovation, even those engagements of biblical narrative that relied on reading a written text presupposed that reading required performance before an actual audience. Recent work in performance criticism has attempted to take the oral origins of biblical narrative seriously (see the chapter by Rhoads). This essay joins in that attempt, exploring in particular the ethical dimensions of biblical narrative that can be discovered through performance.

Music Doesn't Fit on Paper

First, some preliminary considerations:

If all engagement with biblical narratives in their culture (and time) of origin presupposes live performance, then the Gospels as we have them are not texts, properly considered, but sheet music. They are recorded cues, recorded in abstract notation, that allow performers to embody the story so that the music may resound.

Recently I was making this point to a group with whom I was studying. I showed the group a piece of sheet music and asked them if they knew what it was. One person, ever devoted to stating the obvious, said, "Well, we know that it is music." The group laughed and agreed. Some in the group, looking at the abstractions on the page, determined that, whatever it was, it had been written for the French horn. The difference in key signature between the solo line and the piano accompaniment was a dead giveaway, they said. This explanation puzzled many in the audience, but we proceeded with our investigation. When someone pointed out that it was classical music, some in the group concluded that this meant only that they would never hear it on the radio. Others knew that this was a judgment based on harmonic structure and the flow of the melody. A few people started humming the melody line, and someone guessed that Mozart had written the piece. They were correct.

I then asked two musicians in the room, a hornist and a pianist, to perform the piece, which was the beginning of the second movement of Mozart's Fourth Concerto for French Horn. Everything changed. Where the music-on-paper had separated people in the room into small groups of music-readers and non-readers, key-signature-readers and non-readers,

readers of music history and non-readers, the experience of hearing the music performed linked all of us together. Even those in the room who could not read at all reacted to the sound, the melody, the flow, and development of the piece of music. When I asked the group to look again at the sheet music with which we had started, someone said, "That was just paper; it wasn't music until they played it. There's a difference." She was right.

This judgment, shared by all in the group (especially the trained musicians who could read the music very well on their own and silently), was telling and important. The reality of music was not exhausted (or even adequately expressed) by the abstract notation with which we began. Physical performance is required before music is really music. Music is not a set of intellectual ciphers; it must physically move the membranes and cilia in the ears.

And the reality of music does not stop with the moving of membranes and cilia. One member of the study group commented that the air in the room was changed by having carried that particular set of vibrations. He was right. There was surely something different in the room, something palpable, something enduring. That "something" was music.

It wasn't just the ears and the air that were involved, however. With performers in the room, the audience was affected visually as well. They could see the eyes of the performers as they went grey and focused, having lent their light to the sound and the effort of performance. They could see the way the music required the pianist to dance, swaying and shifting, swirling as the notes ran on the keyboard. They could see the horn player lift her chin during a lilting line, or move her hand into the bell of her horn to darken the sound, or shift her feet as she prepared to play. This visual dance was also part of the music.

There is a difference between paper and music, and everyone in the room knew it. Music does not fit on paper; it is not merely an intellectual abstraction; it is not even simply sounds. To be music, the performance had to "take place." Watch that metaphor carefully. It means that music, to really be music, must be recognized and experienced as a spatial reality affecting our ears and our eyes, affecting all the senses by which we orient ourselves in space. Music, to really be music, cannot be simply an intellectual reality. It is not even enough for it to be an aural reality. The performance that we heard had to "take place," that is to say that it had to take up actual space, and this occupying of space was crucial to the reality of the music.

Stories Also Have to Take Up Space

The same thing is true for storytelling. A text is not a story until it is performed by a storyteller, and only when it is performed can it actually take place. And the only way it can take place is to take up space.

If the story is performed by a solo performer, the story takes up space, in much the same way that music takes up space when performed by a soloist. The audience sits here; the soloist/storyteller stands there, and the performance begins. Seeing and hearing the performance (while sharing the same space) changes everything. An audience can listen to any number of recorded performances and still be surprised by what happens when a tenor sends a high C soaring into the air above the audience. The people in the audience see the way the music affects the person who is performing it. They see the breathing, the lifting of the chin, the fire in the eyes, the tender tilt of the head. This is the case for both musicians and storytellers, performers all. Everything that an audience sees and hears takes up space when it takes place.

But storytellers do something more. Because theirs is an explicitly narrative art form, less abstract than even the most narrational of programmed music, they must follow the story they are telling as it moves through the imagined spatial world of the story. They follow the story from here to there, and as they do, everything changes. The audience is still in the same single room with the storyteller, and mostly they are sitting quite still, but the story has just moved, and the storyteller has brought the audience along, through space, to cause this to take place.

And then the storyteller does even more: when she meets new characters inside the story, she has to create a plausible conversation between these characters. For these characters to converse, one must stand here and the other over there. (This is, of course, a consequence of simple physics: two entities cannot occupy the same space or they are no longer two entities, but one.) Still there is only one voice, but now that voice must create the separation between the two characters. Now the voice must take up the space that expresses the difference (and maybe disagreement) between the two characters. An audience can, of course, see that there is only one body before them, and can hear that there is only one voice, but part of the joy of participating (as audience) in a performance comes with granting the storyteller the power to create multiple characters who meet each other in space. We accept the differences in voice and place as real even though we see and hear only a soloist. We accept them as real because we know that stories have to take up space, if only in our imaginations.

Taking Up Space with More Than One Body

It is, of course, a natural development to take the dramatic stories of the Bible and perform them as dramas. Shimon Levy argues that this development is natural even in Jewish culture, which distrusted (historically) theatrical representation as much as it distrusted representation in the plastic arts.[1] Biblical narratives are strong narratives with great tension and clash, great dramatic potential. It is natural that they should find dramatic representation, but something happens when you move from solo storytelling to ensemble dramatic presentation. In particular, space happens.

Space happens because drama (usually) requires more than one body. And with more than one body, voices originate from more than one point. A point, by definition, has no area, no volume, and takes up no space. Once you have two, or three, or four actors on stage, space happens, since two points make a line, three non-co-linear points make a plane, and four non-co-planar points make three dimensional space.

For more than a decade, I have worked with an ensemble of storytellers, a troupe of actors that works together to perform the stories that we study. That means that for more than a decade I have had the privilege of discovering these stories in the space between the bodies of the actors onstage. Everything changes when you work with an ensemble. In particular, space changes. In our work together, we have therefore had to take up the matter of space and its interpretive consequences.

Once the story is discovered in space, it can really "take place." The metaphor may be old and tired, but it still carries force. Anything that actually happens and has an effect in the world has its effect because it takes place, because it seizes space in the world where physical forces have

1. Shimon Levy, *The Bible as Theatre* (Sussex: Sussex Academic 2002).

physical consequences. The "seizing" metaphor is worth noting, but so is the fact that what is seized is "place." This matters, because anything that really exists does so because it stands out in a particular place, the place that it has taken. This matters because anything that is no place is no thing. And nothing has no effect on the world we live in, the world of interlocking physical causes. (Note the trouble that Polyphemos had with Odysseus around just such a linguistic matter.[2]) The converse is also true: a story that is performed in space, a story that "takes place," can have a real, and powerful, effect on the world of physical causes into which we are woven.

The Basics of Ensemble Performance in Space: Bodies and Faces

For the scenes in a performed gospel to take place, they must take up space. That means, in the first place, that someone is going to have to stand here, and someone else is going to have to stand there. These are physical realities, with physical consequences that affect interpretation. The characters in the scene are going to have to face each other, or not, move toward each other or away. Characters will be near to each other, or far away, or they will move until they are far too close to each other. Each of these choices will, in turn, have physical and interpretive consequences, and these consequences will be felt by the members of the audience.

Because of these consequences, an ensemble of performers will have to decide how the scene will take up space. If the two characters in the scene circle each other warily, this lends a certain bite to the words of the scene. If the two characters lean together, touch foreheads, and talk quietly, this way of using space makes the scene intimate, maybe even tender. Of course, if these same characters assume the same position, only this time they yell their lines and move their hands sharply and aggressively through space, the scene is very different.

When an ensemble performs together, one must not just take up space and consider the physics of bodies, one must also confront the matter of faces. Each actor comes equipped with one, and the characters in a

---

2. Odysseus, held captive in the cave of the Cyclops, gave his name as "No Man." When Polyphemos called out for help because "No Man" had wounded him, his neighbors concluded that nothing had happened because no one had done anything.

scene will some time encounter each other face to face. When that happens, space again changes and transforms.

The philosopher Emmanuel Levinas argues that human life is born in the discovery of the face of an other. In particular, ethics is born in the space between face and face, and ethics is what makes human life human.[3] Ethics is born, says Levinas, because in the face of the other I encounter one whom I cannot control and must not kill.

Many years ago, more than half my life, just before my wife and I were to marry, I asked an old pastor (ninety at the time) what I needed to know about being married. He and his wife had just celebrated their sixty-fifth wedding anniversary, so I figured that he might know something that would be helpful to me as a soon-to-be-married person. Pastor Mueller rolled his eyes as he often did when I asked a question for which there was no answer. Finally he said, "Here's all that I know about marriage: I wake up in the morning, I roll over and I look at my wife, and I realize that I have absolutely no idea what she is going to do next." At the time (in my infinite wisdom), I thought that this was not much of an answer. Now, after 33 years of marriage (and after reading Levinas) Pastor Mueller looks wiser and wiser. It is indeed in the discovery of the uncontrollable face of the other that human life takes place, and the ethical shape of human life is determined by how the tense space between face and face is bridged, whether by a caress or by a blow or by a touch of consolation or compromise.

The same thing is true onstage. The characters that carry the dramatic potential of the biblical story now encounter each other in space, not in textual abstraction. Once the characters encounter each other in space, they must take up the space that separates them. That is to say that they must engage in the real human activities that make the scene truthful: they must discover each other, explore each other's positions, and negotiate their way to a settling of the matters that take place between them. So, for instance, when the actor plays the part of a mother who searches for Jesus and finds him, a mother whose daughter is possessed by a demon, a mother who is a Gentile, a Syro-Phoenician by birth (Mark 7:24–32), she must invent a way to cross the space between herself and Jesus, and the way she negotiates this crossing must be believable to an audience that knows a great deal about how such a negotiation must take place.

3. Emmanuel Levinas, *Totality and Infinity: An Essay on Exteriority*, trans. Alphonso Lingis (Pittsburgh: Duquesne University Press, 1969).

These physical negotiations carry the (often unspoken) ethical tension of any scene, especially when the scene involves characters who touch each other in the course of the scene. Onstage as in life, touch is powerful, life-changing, dramatic, and so, onstage as in life, characters negotiate touch carefully. They touch each other or they refuse touch in every human interaction. Jacques LeCoq, a drama theorist and trainer of actors, says that finally all of human life comes down to pulling and pushing.[4] It all comes down to touching or not touching, accepting or refusing. This is true onstage and in all of life. Consider the scenes where Jesus lays his hands on children to bless them. A solo storyteller may tell this story and focus only on the fact of the blessing. This is quite understandable, since the blessing is a central idea in the scene. Onstage, however, the performers and the audience have to see and share the negotiations that are involved in gaining permission to touch someone else's children. Even if the mothers bring the children with the express purpose of having Jesus touch them, still no one touches a child without first gaining confirmed permission. Performers will do this by negotiating face-to-face, and the audience will see it and experience its reality. Conversely, if the actor playing Jesus were to skip the ritual of face-to-face negotiation, an audience would experience the scene as an invasion, or even as an assault, surely not the interpretive line that the original storyteller intended.

Taking Up Space in Mark's Story: Mark 5:21–43

Jesus has climbed out of a boat. Someone, moving from far away and coming close, falls at Jesus' feet. The person who came from there to here, the person now kneeling before Jesus, his head lower, is named Jairus, and his daughter is at the point of death. He has come from his house out to the sea to bring Jesus back to the house, to bring him into the house, to bring him into the room inside the house where the little girl lies, nearly dead. The father has come to bring Jesus back so that he can touch the child and heal her.

Jesus goes with him. When he turns to go with him back to the house, space changes. Jesus moves through a crowd that crushes up against him. This is touch that means nothing, though it slows him down.

4. Jacques LeCoq, *The Moving Body*, trans. David Bradby (New York: Routledge, 2001).

I was in a New York subway car at rush hour. When the car started, everyone swayed together, pulling and pushing those around them. From all over the car, people mumbled apologies. The responses came also from all over the car: "That's okay, honey." The touch was insignificant, both in the subway car and on the way to Jairus' house. Now Jesus, along with the large crowd that crushes up against him, is moving purposefully through space, taking the short route, moving quickly. He is on a mission, and you can tell it from the way he moves through space. All of space becomes a straight line from here to there, and all of time becomes an hourglass through which the little girl's life drains as Jesus moves toward her. He may run out of time.

Of course, dogmatic interpretation will have none of this. There is no drama in dogma, only demonstration of static truths that must be defended. Dogmatic interpretation knows that Jesus will heal the little girl, and it tolerates the story only because the story can be told to demonstrate that Jesus has complete control over everything. That's why dogma doesn't take up space.

But as an ensemble of storytellers embodies this story, dogma has to wait while Jesus moves through space. The story requires it. This has to take time, and Jesus may run out of time. That is the spatial reality of the story.

Jesus moves through space, pushing through the crushing crowd.

And then a woman comes. As soon as she enters the space around Jesus, the story slows down. We are introduced to her and to her malady. We are drawn into the endless, exhausting flow of her attempts to be healed. We discover, as she swims upstream behind Jesus, that she has nothing left and that her condition has grown worse. And then the storyteller swirls us into the woman's thinking. She is swimming through the crowd because she has heard about Jesus. She is swimming behind him because she wanted to come close enough to Jesus to touch him, to touch even the hem of his garment, to cross that final bit of space that separates her from him and touch him. She expects that this crossing of space will rescue her.

She is right.

When she touches him, time and space are punctured, and the crush of insignificant touch vanishes under the impact of the one significant touch in the whole crushing crowd. When she touches Jesus, the woman knows that she has been healed.

When she touches him, Jesus knows that he has been touched. The storyteller tells us that he felt the *dunamis* go out of him, that power that in some contexts is translated to refer to all sorts of potency (including sexual), and an ancient audience would have been reminded of the cultural notion that a menstruating woman might possess the power to curdle milk and sap a man's potency. Now the story slows down even more. Jesus no longer moves purposefully through space toward the little girl. He turns and turns, around in the crowd. He keeps saying, "Who touched my clothing?" He keeps looking for the woman who had done this. The woman who swam through the crowded space behind Jesus, trying to touch him, the woman who has been healed, sees Jesus dithering, swirling, and stopping. She sees the crowd milling and losing its purpose. She comes from her place behind Jesus and falls down before him.

Now come the words that dogmatists love. Jesus hears the whole truth. He announces that the healing took place because of faithfulness. Truth and faithfulness are things that dogma imagines it can manage, and (with time) it will find a way to make the healing take up as little earthly space as does dogmatically imagined salvation.

But then people come from the house of Jairus, and they re-establish the pull of the place Jesus was going before he started turning and turning around in the crowd, the pull of the mission that enveloped Jesus before he starting dithering and ran out of time. "Your daughter has died," they say. "Why bother the teacher any longer?"

Time stops, and space is frozen.

Of course, none of this bothers dogmatists. They still know that Jesus will heal the little girl. They still know the disembodied truth that makes everything okay.

This is the moment that space and embodiment of the story make all the difference. In a page-text, being read silently, the woman with the hemorrhage vanishes and becomes an obscured memory as the abstract text moves on to its conclusion. If a soloist is performing the scene, the woman diminishes and winks out like a star in the morning sky as the soloist turns from what has just happened and engages in the new mission. The audience may remember the place where they last could see the star, they may (to shift the metaphor) feel the bump as they run over the seam between scene and scene, but still everyone goes on to the dogmatic conclusion for which we have all been waiting. But if an ensemble is performing the scene, the bump is harder to cruise over. In fact, the bump stops the scene cold. A living body onstage is durable and cannot simply vanish when the story moves on.

When the messengers come from the house of Jairus, the storyteller tells us that they come while Jesus was still speaking to the woman who swam up behind him in the crowd. This moment of shocking discovery happens while Jesus is still speaking to the woman. She is still kneeling before him on the ground. She is still looking him in the face, puzzled perhaps as to why Jesus had chosen to mill the herd just to create this moment of face-to-face encounter. And since she is still kneeling there, her face open to the audience, she hears the words spoken by the messenger. The words mean something to her that they would mean to no one else: the girl died because she touched Jesus and set him swirling and spinning aimlessly.

An actor in an ensemble has to decide what happens to the woman's face at such a moment. Is she appalled? Is she crushed? Is she unaffected because, after all, she got what she came for? Is she angry that the girl died because Jesus, for some untraceable reason, needed to cease moving toward the little girl's house in order to dither in the crowd? There are many possibilities, and all of them mean something different in the space between her face and Jesus' face.

Because the actor portraying the woman has a face that the audience can see, the audience learns something about this scene that they might well have missed had the story taken up less space. At the least, the audience has to consider what it means that Jesus dithers until a little girl dies. More significantly, the audience is handed the expansive theological task of figuring out what it means for the messiah to come and leave death and Rome still in place, still in power, still dominating life in God's creation. Dogmatists may sit calmly with their answers, but an audience who has seen the woman's face, and felt the strained tension in the space between her and Jesus, will not be able to sit so calmly. An audience that has seen the reality of the woman's face, embodied in space, will find itself caught in the crucial task of puzzling out the problems posed by a messiah who does not turn the whole creation right-side-up, but instead is crucified in a world that continues (even after the messiah arrives) to starve children to death or kill their parents in genocidal conflicts.

This is not simply a theological difficulty. Performance in space reveals that this is a matter of ethics and action. What is it that moves Jesus back toward his original mission? Is it the look of horror on the face of the woman who had been healed? Does her face scold him into remembering what he was supposed to be doing? Or does he shrug off her reaction since he (like the dogmatists) knows exactly what he's going to do? Is Jesus surprised when the messengers come from the house of Jairus? Was he so immersed in finding the woman who had touched him that he lost track of all else? If so, what does his face do when he hears the report of the girl's death?

Each of these questions spurs ethical reflection. That is not surprising. Once you take the notion of Incarnation seriously, once you grant to Jesus a human body as real as those bodies around him, you must examine each of Jesus' actions with an eye to ethics, since ethics concerns itself with the interactions of bodies in space. Once you study the scenes in the gospels as interactions among bodies in ethical space, you find surprise after surprise. The woman who had been healed of the malady in her body, hears the messengers and the audience sees her reaction. The father of the little girl sees Jesus divert from his purposeful course and his face also reacts. Such reactions are governed by the physics of real human interaction and are judged by ethical considerations. Once you grant real human bodies both to Jesus and to the people around him, you have to grant them faces that see each other, faces also that the audience sees.

This applies throughout Mark's gospel. It's not just the woman and the father who have faces that react. The mother who negotiates a healing for her daughter in 7:24–32 is called a dog, right to her face. How does her face react to this insult? More difficult still, what does Jesus' face look like when he says these insulting words? Or what look passes between the face of Jesus and the face of the woman who anoints his head (14:1–10), thus making him the Anointed One in the Gospel of Mark? Or what happens to the faces of the women who come to anoint his corpse at the end of the story, come expecting to see a dead face that does not look back or react as they tend it one last time? Or what does it mean that the story ends with no one, not the women, not the disciples, not even the reader ever seeing the face of the risen Jesus? All of these questions provide new challenges for interpreters that take up the matter of space when considering how the scenes in the gospel take place.

Working with an ensemble of actors gives you the gift of space, but that gift comes with demands. Once you take up space as an aid to interpretation, you cannot simply retreat to the static spiritual answers provided by dogmatic interpretation. Once you take the incarnation seriously, you have to honor the physical meanings that emerge from the faces that mark the space between them and Jesus.

This is a demanding gift, but it is a productive one.

Questions and Exercises

1. Describe how you have experienced live music at a concert or other venue. How does Swanson's description of music resonate with your experience? What does this say about the performance of biblical texts?

2. Look back at the section where the author describes various face changes between Jesus and the healed woman. Stage these moments with someone else, trying out the various ways their faces might have changed. What do you learn about this story by this simple practice of taking up space with another?

3. What differences and similarities do you see between the method used by Swanson's troupe and the descriptions of other styles of performance in this volume? What does each style of performance offer that the others may not?

10

PERFORMING THE LIVING WORD
Learnings from a Storytelling Vocation

DENNIS DEWEY

EARLY IN THE FIRST YEAR OF MY SEMINARY EDUCATION, I had a vivid dream in which I was a participant in an archeological dig in the Judean wilderness. To my astonishment the dream culminated in my discovery of the "Dead Sea Tapes"—ancient audio recordings of the Scriptures! I awoke from the dream in fits of laughter and shared with my colleagues this silly anachronism. Many such dreams "die at the opening day," as Isaac Watts' Psalm paraphrase attests, but this one I could not shake off. The strange experience impressed itself on my memory so that when, nearly a decade and a half later, I discerned a call to biblical storytelling as my life's work, I began to understand that dream as prophetic validation. For three decades now I have been telling the stories of Scripture—half of those years spent in a full time ministry of storytelling.[1]

Beginnings

On my first Palm Sunday as a parish pastor, I decided to perform the passion narrative from Mark's gospel (Mark 14–15) as a "dramatic monologue." (With a background in theater, I still thought of the performance of biblical text as acting. The nomenclature of "biblical storytelling" and my self-identification as "a biblical storyteller" would await my meeting Tom Boomershine). That Palm Sunday "telling" was more powerful and

1. www.DennisDewey.org.

stirring than I had anticipated. Its enthusiastic reception by parishioners was evidenced in genuine, heartfelt responses. All were moved. Some wept. Many said, "I have never heard *anything* like that!" Others asked, "Where did you get that *script*?" I was struck that some did not recognize as Scripture the word-for-word performance of Mark's text. The congregation's hearing the powerful and dramatic text in that way bore little resemblance to their customary experience of Scripture readings as dead, dull, and dusty. Suddenly, the Bible was not an antique museum piece to be revered, explicated, and ensconced in a display case; they had felt the word in the *solar plexus*.

The following year I registered for a continuing education event called "The Gospel as Storytelling" with a professor of New Testament named Thomas Boomershine. Over the several evenings of that seminar, Tom told the whole of Mark's gospel. Inspired by Boomershine's example, I resolved to learn the chapters that led up to the passion narrative I had already performed. I used the method of "internalization" that Boomershine taught. From that first study I learned that the acquisition of text as sacred memory was older than Scripture itself, that even the word "text," commonly used to denote written or printed words, carries in its etymology the oral roots of "weaving a tale" or "spinning a yarn" (texture, textile). My appreciation for the differences between oral and literate culture began to inform my understanding of Scripture.

Boomershine helped me understand that the ancient, oral world thought differently from the literate world of the academy in which I had done biblical studies—in short, that that world thought in story. This insight was to shape my work profoundly, both as a performer and itinerant pedagogue. Most literate people regard oral culture as "backward." As people educated in institutions that virtually equate literacy with learning, we carry with us an almost viral assumption that education always required literacy. My slow shedding of this bias was the first stage of a dawning appreciation of the storied, oral culture of Jesus (who, it must be observed, never wrote a book). This evolving understanding of the role of storytelling in oral culture helped both validate my sense of call to this ministry and value storytelling as urgent and timely.

Boomershine further reminded me that theater/drama and storytelling are distinctive *genres* with different aesthetics and different histories. Theater's aesthetic is indirect, the aesthetic of illusion, which entails the shared suspension of disbelief as the audience pretends that the action on stage is real and the actors pretend that no audience is present. Storytelling's aesthetic, on the other hand, is direct. The storyteller is the storyteller. The storyteller looks at the audience. The audience interacts with the storyteller. The storyteller as narrator relates directly to the audience. There is no "illusion" save the transient adoption of a character by the storyteller in dialogue. The energy exchange between storyteller and listener is palpable and immediate. Theater's energy is indirect, mediate, askew, not face-to-face.

Theater was ubiquitous in the Roman period,[2] but Jesus almost certainly did not attend. Theater was associated with the Greco-Roman culture and religions. The Jews, who had little visual art because of the proscription against graven images, had storytelling as the centerpiece of their culture. With Boomershine's help, I began to think of myself no longer as an actor/dramatist, but rather as an artist in continuity with a performance tradition of even greater antiquity: storytelling.

As notice of my performance of the Gospel of Mark spread, the invitations to perform it increased. I began to integrate biblical storytelling with my pastoral work and with parish worship. When my third pastorate came to be characterized by persistent conflict, I underwent a career counseling process that surfaced the discernment that, in the best of all possible worlds, my vocation would be "biblical storyteller." Yet this presented challenged in terms of the practical needs of my family. We had two young children and soon another on the way. To make a long story short, my family took the leap together and I became a full-time biblical storyteller and itinerate teacher. This vocation spanned the next fifteen years, taking me to churches, colleges, festivals, seminars, conferences and similar venues in thirty-nine states with more than two dozen denominations as well as to Canada, Korea, New Zealand, South Africa, the United Kingdom, Israel/Palestine, Greece, Spain, and Turkey. The culmination of this ministry came when I co-mentored a Doctor of Ministry group in biblical storytelling with my mentor-now-colleague and friend, Tom Boomershine.

---

2 See L. L. Welbourne, *Paul, the Fool of Christ: A Study of 1 Corinthians 1–4 in the Comic-Philosophic Tradition*, Early Christianity in Context (London: T. & T. Clark, 2005).

Networks of Support

At this same time I became involved with the organization Boomershine had formed with his colleague, Adam (Gil) Bartholomew: The Network of Biblical Storytellers. "NOBS" became for me the nexus of many rewarding personal relationships as well as the matrix of my developing skills and deepening understanding of my craft, art, and spiritual discipline. Working with and for the Network in a variety of capacities over the years, I came to appreciate the variety of approaches to biblical storytelling and to the ways in which telling the stories can have profound effects on tellers and listeners.

A regular feature of the Annual NOBS Festival Gathering is the "Epic Telling," a communal effort at performing at one sitting a whole book or major portion of a book from the Bible. Over the years these Epic Tellings included the Gospel of Mark, the Gospel of Matthew, the Gospel of Luke, the Joseph Cycle, the first half of Genesis, Esther coupled with the Letter of James, the first part of Acts, and other major pieces of Scripture. Without fail, the response at the conclusion of these tellings was exhausted elation—a lot of hugging and high-fiving and a sense that we had together witnessed something as ancient and profound as it was current and inspiring. Working first as a consultant to the board of NOBS and then as the organization's Executive Director, all of our administrative work was always undertaken in the context of learning and telling to one another the stories of Scripture. The deep, caring relationships developed in the Network were "storied" relationships—formed, nurtured, lived out in the context of this art form and spiritual discipline. Those of us who participated in the NOBS community knew the power and creative energy behind performing the text as story—what our British friends refreshingly called "text telling." To those who had never experienced it, however, the thought of "merely reciting" the words of Scripture seemed like a rather dull enterprise. "Where is the creativity in that?" they would demand. So I formulate this "provisional" definition to capture the sense of this art form:

> Biblical Storytelling a spiritual discipline which entails the lively interpretation, expression and animation of a narrative text of the Old or New Testaments which has first been deeply internalized and is then remembranced,[3] embodied, breathed and voiced by

---

3. I coined the term "remembranced" to reflect the mysterious reality experienced in storytelling whereby the events of the past become present in the telling. The term

a teller/performer as a sacred event in community with an audience/congregation.

But a *definition* of something (say, sex, for example) is not the same thing as (and often a poor substitute for) the *experience* of that thing. I soon learned that talking about biblical storytelling was a poor strategy. The best approach began with the invitation, "Let me tell you a story."

Gleanings

Among the important *learnings* that I have gleaned from the biblical storytelling life is how traditional exegesis has failed to appreciate the humor in so many of the stories of Scripture. How could something that was so much fun be so important? Short answer: Perhaps "important" and "fun" are not mutually exclusive categories. I cannot help but think that Elijah's enigmatic response to Elisha's request for a portion of the spirit double of that given to the other prophets. I can only understood this in light of its comedic sense. "You have asked a hard thing; yet, if you see me as I am being taken from you, it will be granted you; if not, it will not," says Elijah (2 Kgs 2:10). My storyteller's sense tells me that this assertion in the classically structured story must be understood with tongue in cheek as if to say, "If you *happen* to be around, this can be done." (Of course Elisha will be around! Despite three consecutive attempts by his mentor to warn him away, Elisha has stuck to him like glue, following him from Gilgal to Bethel, from Bethel to Jericho and from Jericho across the Jordan!)

The pointed humor of the blind man in John 9 always gets a laugh when he says to his interrogators, who persist in questioning how he has regained his sight, "*Hhhhhhhhh,* [storyteller's exasperated breath added] I've told you already; why do you want to hear it again? Do you want to be his disciples, too?" In Mark's gospel the dimwitted response of the disciples to Jesus' feeding of the 4,000 (despite their having just witnessed his multiplication of the loaves and fishes for the 5,000) sets up the comedy-of-errors-in-the-boat story that follows as Jesus blows off steam to them about his encounter with the Pharisees, and they misunderstand him to be citing the fact that they have forgotten to bring bread with them (8:14–21). The rubric implicit in the storytelling structure of

---

is deliberate in its association with the words of institution in the Eucharist, "Do this in *remembrance* of me."

Matthew's genealogy (1:1–17) demands that the third and final repetition of "fourteen generations" belongs to the audience; when I perform it that way, the release of energy is always marked by the hearers' knowing smiles and chuckling sighs. That we have managed to squash the humor out of these stories is a consequence of reading them as Scripture instead of hearing them as stories.

The overall effect of having these stories "by heart" and hearing them come alive has been for me to discern the radical openness of grace, the power of forgiveness, and the joy that is God's intention for all life. My career as a biblical storyteller has led me to the realization that mine is a sheltered and protected life. I feel the call of God to move out of that and into more vulnerable/available spirituality that is enacted in mission. Some of the most truly spiritual moments of my storytelling ministry have been telling, in Spanish, Mark's story of Jesus calming the sea to a group of Mayan children outside their thatched hut in Copan, Honduras, and telling in Afrikaans, to a mixed race congregation in South Africa, the story of Jesus washing of the disciples feet, and telling the passion narrative from John's Gospel during Holy Week in a Houston street mission. Having the stories by heart, I have come to believe, was the core activity of spiritual development for ancient Israel and the early church. I hold this conviction as much by dint of experience as by the fruits of my research.

My work and faith as a biblical storyteller has led to some profound changes in my understanding of canon. Perhaps it is not too extreme an opinion to venture (from a purely socio-historical point of view) that Jesus of Nazareth would have had a problem with the notion of canon that evolved following his time on earth. I can easily imagine that Jesus the storyteller would resist the codification of the stories of his ministry into four gospels and the further collection of those into a "New Testament" of the "Holy Bible." All that I have learned from living with Jesus in his stories points in another direction—*away* from the tendency to "build booths" (Mark 9:5), to enforce limits (Mark 9:40; Luke 13:10–17), and fix boundaries (John 4:7–42). Storytelling has helped me come to see rigid religion as potentially inimical to true faith. My storied spirituality has moved me toward skepticism about truth claims expressed in purely propositional form—particularly those which are exclusive. Storytelling the biblical texts has made me less tolerant of doctrinaire religion, which often substitutes its system for the creating, living God. Important truth is always rich, usually paradoxical and often ironic, and so is best expressed in story, in metaphor, in acts of kindness, in the wonder of silence, in active listening.

I am often repulsed by the ideas, words, and actions of those who identify themselves as "Christian." I wonder if reclaiming the storyteller who is "the pioneer and perfecter of our faith" (Heb 12:2) might just temper the obsessive-compulsive disorder that so often masquerades as Christianity in our culture. With Parker Palmer, "I find it hard to name my beliefs using traditional Christian language because that vocabulary has been taken hostage by theological terrorists and tortured beyond recognition."[4] Storytelling has moved me in my own faith journey toward the edge, and there, ironically, I believe, to find the center.

The Medium of the Spoken Word

All this began for me when Boomershine's initial insight about original orality of Scripture set me on a course of research, reflection, teaching, and performing. Over the course of those years, I came to understand that most of what we, as literate people, think about the Bible as a literary document is not only wrong but 180 degrees from right. This critique of our "documentary bias" became the dominant emphasis in my teaching the theory, practice, art, and spiritual discipline of biblical storytelling.

The "word" in Scripture almost always refers to the spoken word. God *said,* "Let there be light"; God did not write it. Spoken words have power. They do things. They accomplish purposes. They happen in time. The written/printed text, as we have it in the Bible, is a transcript of a performance, the fossil record of a lively storytelling tradition. This understanding helps the practitioner of biblical storytelling to approach this performance art as "recovery" or "discovery" of what is already in the text. The performer does not interpolate, embellish, or elaborate. The biblical storyteller is not a redecorator, but rather is a spelunker, going deep into the text.

I once asked my grandmother what it was like for her as a child, when her family first had the house wired for electricity. Her response surprised and puzzled me. "My whole world," she said, "suddenly became dark." I had assumed, of course, that the technological "improvement" of

---

4. Parker Palmer, *The Promise of Paradox: A Celebration of the Contradictions in the Christian Life* (San Francisco: Jossey-Bass, 2008) xxi.

electrical service would have done just the opposite. But she explained to me that, before electricity, the house was supplied with gas lights. At dusk her father would light all the lights of the house, and the house was filled with light. But when the house was wired and each room had its own incandescent bulb hanging from a wire, her father made her turn out the light when she left a room. So much for my assumptions about the advent of electricity! The direction in which Boomershine pointed me led to me to believe that most of what document-based scholarship has concluded is similarly misguided through the systematically projecting backwards of its tacit assumptions about the technology of literacy.

The high-literate approach to the stories of Scripture may be more obscuring than enlightening. The significant gains made possible by the technologies of literacy had a shadow side. Downloading the communal memory to storage on inked pages represented a change in the relationship of story to community. Plato's Socrates gave expression to this in the *Phaedrus*:

> [T]his discovery of yours [writing] will create forgetfulness in the learners' souls, because they will not use their memories; they will trust to the external written characters and not remember of themselves. The specific which you have discovered is an aid not to memory, but to reminiscence, and you give your disciples not truth, but only the semblance of truth; they will be hearers of many things and will have learned nothing; they will appear to be omniscient and will generally know nothing; they will be tiresome company, having the show of wisdom without the reality.[5]

The ancient philosopher's misgivings about the shift from oral to literate communication finds resonance with some of the attitudes that attend the shift from a literate a digital culture. In her recent study of the reading brain, Maryanne Wolf cites this parallel:

> [Q]uestions raised more than two millennia ago by Socrates about literacy address many concerns of the early twenty-first century. I came to see that Socrates' worries about the transition from an oral culture to a literate one and the risks it posed, especially for young people, mirrored my own concerns about the immersion of our children into a digital world. Like the ancient Greeks we are embarked on a powerfully important transition—in our case from a written culture to one that is more digital and visual.

5. Plato *Phaedo* 274–75. Online: http://www.gutenberg.org/dirs/etext99/phdrs10.txt.

> I regard the fifth and fourth centuries BCE, when Socrates and Plato taught, as a window through which our culture can observe a different but no less remarkable culture making an uncertain transition from one dominant mode of communication to another.[6]

I write the present essay aboard a ship in the Aegean Sea as I lead a group on a biblical storytelling pilgrimage. We have just departed Kusadasi, Turkey, having spent the afternoon touring ancient Ephesus. In the shade trees adjacent to the ancient port and in view of the theater that was already old in Paul's time, we heard the story of the riot of the silversmiths (Acts 19:21–41). Again, the listeners were moved by the power and energy of the spoken word—not read from the page, but recited by heart, told as though coming from inside the teller as indeed it was. In this place, I am reminded of the connection of memory to spoken language and storytelling, and see the parallels behind the shifts in the culture of ancient Greece and those of the biblical tradition.

> For centuries the stories that Homer drew on to create his epics had been sustained by oral tradition and held in the memories of the *aoidoi* [singer-poets]. But with the ancient stories being written down, life was going out of them. . . . Memory had been the chief gift and instrument of the *aoidos*. Not the short-term memory of retaining stories from a written document to be recited the next day, but a memory that spanned generations and held the inheritance as a sacred trust, for otherwise it would be lost. Memory personified in Greek thought was the mother of the Muses . . .
>
> Once the storyteller's lore was written down and sealed forever in the letters of the written word, the Muses became dispensable. The strong feeling was that the Muses departed when the words were written and with them the authority that verified and testified to the myths and folk tales as recited by the inspired *aoidos*.[7]

The rediscovery of the vitality of the oral tradition, learning the stories as sounds and images, telling the stories with passion and excitement was illuminating—not with the glaring incandescent glow of the bare bulb, but with the warm, suffusing glow of the flame.

6. Maryanne Wolf, *Proust and the Squid: The Story and Science of the Reading Brain* (New York: HarperCollins, 2007) 70.

7. John Harrell, *Origins and Early Traditions of Storytelling* (Kensington, CA: York, 1983) 47.

Jesus of Nazareth appeared on the historical scene in the midst of a culture that was semi-literate, but fundamentally oral. Some could read, but most did not as there was precious little to be read. As Richard Horsley has observed about the politics of literacy in Galilee of the first century of the common era, the Gospel of Mark pits Jesus and his non-literate entourage against the literate-temple structure. This system was in oppressive cahoots with the Roman occupiers. Literacy is a technology of subjugation, a tool of oppression.[8] Jesus scathingly indicts the scribes, who will "receive greater condemnation" because they use their techno-logical skill to "devour widow's houses" (Mark 12:38–40). It is even within the realm of possibility that Jesus never mastered literacy skills whatso-ever. As John P. Meier notes, "in an oral culture one could theoretically be an effective teacher . . . without engaging in reading or writing. So the question remains: Was Jesus literate or illiterate?"[9]

Furthermore, all of what was read in antiquity was read aloud, usu-ally in public. The very physical act and common understanding of the process reading, as Susan Niditch has convincingly argued, was quite different from what we, as people who live in world of books—50,000 of them newly brought to print each year in the United States alone!—think of as "reading" two millennia later.[10] The two communication systems, oral and literate, interacted with each other—sometimes in symbiosis, sometimes in tension, and often even in conflict with one another. The oral communication of sacred "texts" (a word which, as noted above, originally denoted oral performance) was generally considered to be superior to the written version, in part because the living voice renders the communication an experience of vitality. Papias, bishop of Heiropolis circa 130 C.E. sought to find those still living who had had some ac-quaintance with the first disciples, because, he said, "I did not suppose that what I got from books would help me as much as the living, surviv-ing voice."[11] The oral tradition was considered not only more vital and expressive, but more durable, trustworthy, and even accurate. After all,

8. Richard Horsley, *Hearing the Whole Story: The Politics of Plot in Mark's Gospel* (Louisville: Westminster John Knox, 2001) 198.

9. John P. Meier, *A Marginal Jew* (New York: Doubleday, 1991) 268. See Fowler's chapter in this volume.

10 Susan Nidtich, *Oral World and Written Word: Ancient Israelite Literature*, Library of Ancient Israel (Louisville: Westminster John Knox, 1996).

11 Eusebius *Ecclesiastical History* 3.39.1–4 (Lake, LCL).

a written text could be secretly amended or edited "out of earshot" of the community. One can almost imagine a hypothetical parent of this transitional time exclaiming, "These kids and their books today! When I was a kid, you had to know something! What is the world coming to if you look everything up in a book?"

An echo of this preferential option for the oral may be found in the dialogue between Jesus and the Devil in Luke's account of the temptation in the wilderness (Luke 4:1-13). Jesus counters the first two temptations (to turn stone into bread and to worship the Devil for personal gain) by responding, "It is written . . ." [*gegraptai*]. The Devil then puts him on the peak of the temple wall and invites Jesus to throw himself down, because, the Devil says, "It is *written*, 'God will give his angels charge of you to protect you. . . .'" But Jesus counters with, "It is *said* [*eiretai*] . . ." In other words, "it is said" trumps "it is written." For me, taking seriously the original orality of Scriptures represented paradigm shift not unlike those that from time to time have characterized various other fields of scientific inquiry. I see "variations on the theme of the folktale, 'The Emperor's New Clothes' in which the obvious is overlooked, then rediscovered in a way that makes one wonder, 'How could we not have seen it all along?'"[12] As a seminary-trained pastor, I appreciated the historical-critical method as the basis of solid exegesis; but as a practitioner of storytelling, I came to see this product of Enlightenment scholarship as dried fruit—nutritious, but not particularly delicious. I caution my students to eat enough of it to be healthy, but not to neglect the sweet, juicy experience of trusting the story as it has come to us, ripe and succulent. Its importance is secondary and supplemental to the process of deep internalization of the text, of living with the text inside oneself and living inside the text. As David Rhoads' convincingly cogent argument for a new "performance criticism" of biblical texts suggests and as my own experience as a storyteller attests, it is possible to read and read, and not hear at all.[13] Hearing the stories told well and faithfully is like hearing them "again for the first time." In my workshops I often read a story from Luke's gospel and then tell that same story. When asked to articulate the differences, participants invariably cite that the "telling" is more lively, more memorable, more embodied, more

12. Dennis Dewey, "A Sea Change in Biblical Studies: Biblical Storytelling Scholarship," *The Journal of Biblical Storytelling* (Indianapolis: The Network of Biblical Storytellers, 2006) 48.

13. See David Rhoads' chapter in this volume.

engaging, and much more affective. Although they have just heard the same story read, the telling that follows seems fresh and new. As one participant once described the multi-sensory experience, "Hearing the story *read* is like 'then and there'; hearing and seeing the story told is like 'here and now.'"

Both as storytellers and as story listeners, we relate differently to the texts of Scripture when they are externalized in print and when they are internalized and told. I have come to distinguish between learning in the head and learning in heart. The former I equate with memorization. The latter I call internalization. The distinction is more than semantic. As Daniel Goleman observes, "The emotional/rational dichotomy approximates the folk distinction between 'heart' and 'head'; knowing something is right 'in your heart' is a different order of conviction somehow, a deeper kind of certainty than thinking so with your rational mind."[14]

The spiritual mnemonic is not so much cerebral as it is cardiological. The heart, the center of the person in Hebrew anatomy, is the primary repository for the tradition. The written text is storage, back-up. The touchstone of First Testament spirituality is the *Shema* (Deut 6:4–9), which counsels the story-formed community to teach the stories and commandments of God to the children (catechize), to talk about them constantly (theologize), to wear reminders of them on the wrists and foreheads (symbolize), and to write them on the doorposts and gates (publicize). But the very first instruction that follows the *Shema* is this: "All these things that I command you this day shall be upon your heart" (internalize). The process of "heart learning" is not the same as the rote memorization of words.[15] Rather it entails the deep internalization of images, feelings, complexes of meaning that are "dressed" in the words that have been traditioned to us (in translation) in Scripture. The professional storytelling community eschews word-for-word storytelling. I was once taken to task by one such well-known professional for calling myself a "biblical storyteller." "Storytellers," he argued, "do not memorize scripts;

---

14. Daniel Goleman, *Emotional Intelligence: Why It Can Matter More Than IQ* (New York: Bantam, 1995) 8.

15 Perhaps there is an oblique reference to this in the Apostle Paul, when he contrasts the inferiority of written letters of recommendation to the living, breathing people being recommend (2 Cor 3:1-11). No doubt dictating to an amanuensis this "letter" that was to be recited to the church at Corinth, Paul observes, "The letter kills, but the Spirit [*to pneuma*] gives life" (2 Cor 3:6).

actors do. You are not a storyteller; you're an actor." But of course, I was able to respond, I do not *memorize*. I learn *by heart*—a process that entails deep immersion in the text, the internalization not just of sounds but of feelings, images, complexes of visualizations of setting, character, and narrative structure, all of it "clothed" with the words of the text. The process used by some actors shares some features of what I call "learning by heart" or "internalizing," but typically an actor's lines are "flushed" as new roles are learned. Learning by heart has more staying power, in part because the words are not just spoken, but prayed. The vocalization of the stories is prayer that begins with the breath that first animated humankind. Again reflecting on the resonance for our own time of Plato/Socrates' misgivings about the implications of the shift from orality to literacy, Maryanne Wolf observes:

> Once a year I ask my undergraduate students how many poems they know "by heart"—a curiously lovely, anachronistic phrase. Students of ten years ago knew between five and ten poems; students today know between one and three. This small sample makes me wonder anew about Socrates' seemingly archaic choices. What are the implications for the next generations, who may commit even less to memory—whether it is fewer poems or even, for some, only part of the multiplication tables? What happens to these children when the electricity goes out, the computer breaks down, or the rocket's systems malfunction? What is the difference in the brain's pathways connecting language and long-term memory for our children and the children of ancient Greece?[16]

My "Dead Sea Tapes" dream is now anachronistic in both temporal directions; no one uses tape anymore. But I have learned that there is something post-modern in the pre-modern. The spell-binding experience of story well told, the images that held audiences' imaginations captive for millennia, the movement to a beat that arrested attention and focused it, the community-building phenomenon of the storyteller's weaving virtual reality—all these find receptivity in post-literate culture. Although I have returned to parish ministry and do my performances and workshops on a reduced scale, I continue to see biblical storytelling as the foundation of my ministry—even of my parish ministry. I have become convinced, as I wrote in a new stanza for the hymn "I Love to Tell the Story":

16. Wolf, *Proust and the Squid*, 75.

The church that lies before us is not the church of old;
The changes in world culture demand new vision bold.
The path for being Christian in this post-modern age
Winds through our storytelling—our ancient heritage!
Rejected from the quarry, this cornerstone of glory,
Remains a fresh, new story for ages yet to come.[17]

The Third Century theologian Tertullian famously challenged the philosophical overlay of theology by asking, "What has Athens to do with Jerusalem?" The question for the 21st Century biblical scholarship and practice is "What has the ancient storytelling tradition of Israel and the gospel storytelling tradition of the First Century to do the culture of the iPod, the DVD, mp3 and the God-knows-what-technology-is-next?" Tom Boomershine answered that question for me thirty years ago, and my life in storytelling has confirmed its truth: "Everything."

Questions

1. What major shifts did Dewey's discovery of the original orality of the Scriptures cause in his thinking?

2. What stories, songs, or poems do you know "by heart"? What difference is there between carrying these internally and having them available in written form?

3. What do you think of the author's claim that the performing of stories that dominated the ancient world now speaks to post-modern sensibilities?

17. Dennis Dewey, "I Love to Tell the Story," © 2006 by Dennis Dewey

Epilogue

The Bible in Modern Media and Beyond

11

INTERPRETING THE BIBLE AT THE HORIZON OF VIRTUAL NEW WORLDS[1]

A. K. M. Adam

THE PRECEDING ESSAYS DISCUSS THE EFFECTS THAT VARI-
ous media have created in representing the Bible through the ages; they
demonstrate the benefit of centuries of historical record and retrospective
analysis. This essay, on the other hand, ventures to broach the question
of the effects of media with which we are only just beginning to get ac-
quainted. From the midst of the profound shift that the advent of digital
media has inaugurated, we can begin to make provisional observations
and hesitantly anticipate some of the differences that digital media might
make.

What does the digital future hold for students of the Bible? One
should probably avoid overconfidence when estimating the ramifications
of the World Wide Web, hypertext, online video, digital publishing, social-
network software, and virtual worlds (to name but a few manifestations of
digital culture). After all, who would have understood the ramifications
Europe's discovery of movable type when the first Bibles were printed

---

1. Much of this essay is adapted from "This Is Not A Bible," in *New Paradigms for
Bible Study: The Bible in the Third Millennium*, edited by Robert Fowler, Edith Blumhofer,
and Fernando Segovia (Philadelphia: Trinity, 2004) 3–20; a short passage on "transla-
tion" appeared in "Poaching on Zion: Biblical Theology as Signifying Practice," in
Reading Scripture with The Church, edited by A. K. M. Adam, Stephen Fowl, and Kevin J.
Vanhoozer (Grand Rapids: Baker Academic, 2006) 21–22. My thanks to the American
Bible Society for permission to use the portions of "This Is Not a Bible," and to Baker
Academic for permission to use the portions from "Poaching On Zion."

on Gutenberg's press? Whatever specific changes develop over the years to come, the advent of electronic media will catalyze a complex of circumstances with which biblical scholars in the age of printing have not yet come to terms (even in the face of film and video media), and the dimensions of these new domains of biblical interpretation lie beyond a fog bank, over an unfamiliar horizon.

Lost in Translation

Granted the uncertainty of what we should anticipate, then, we ought probably to bear in mind several ways that digital media differ profoundly from the print media that constitute the basis of conventional modes of interpretation. For instance, digital media involve much greater variety of appearance than do print media. Whereas scholars of the print generation have become accustomed to communicating primarily by means of the words they chose, the explosive breadth of means for communicating information in digital media affords limitless options for enriching interpretation. Academic biblical scholars need to awaken to a range of communicative practices that extends far beyond the print media in which we typically subsist; one might well ask, "If a picture is worth a thousand words, why can't we have more illustrations and fewer multivolume sets in our commentaries?" Once we admit a richer span of communicative options, however, we will need an articulate mode of criticizing these representations.

The circumstances most liable to change in our future resist precise articulation, in part because they are effects of the *structure* of biblical scholarship as academic institutions have defined it. The academic discipline of biblical studies has grown up amid the broad cultural currents of nineteenth- and twentieth-century European and American modernity, at the intersection of divergent, often conflicting, forces driven by theological and secular academic interests. The confluence and divergence of these formative influences has produced an academic field whose central practices and guiding metaphors derive from a particular model of *translation*. The academic biblical scholar tells an audience what the Bible means, how the texts written in ancient Hebrew and Aramaic, and in Hellenistic Greek should be expressed in contemporary European and American vernaculars. Unfortunately, practitioners of academic biblical scholarship do not usually draw on the full wisdom of scholars in the field of translation, nor do they admit the serious limitations of translation as the primary model for interpretation.

Instead of benefiting from the work of theoreticians and practitioners of translation, academic biblical scholarship tends to show a persistent inclination toward a fantasy of a perfect one-word-to-one-word equivalence. However sophisticated one's theory of translation, however erudite one's grasp of the subtleties of Greek and Hebrew, Latin and Aramaic, when one prepares a translation one eventually must select a single expression in the target language to correspond to the expression in the original, ancient text. A translator does not usually enjoy the liberty to translate the preface to Luke's gospel as,

> Inasmuch as many have set their hands, really sort of "tried," if you know what I mean, to compile, or put together, a narrative concerning the things that have taken place—really, "fulfilled" as you might say—among us, just as those who were eyewitnesses or who became ministers of the word handed them down to us, I too figured that after having followed everything precisely in order from the beginning, to write for you (most excellent Theophilus, which means "Godlover"), in order that you might learn (with overtones of "recognize") about the things you have been instructed, the certainty—or "you might learn the secure facts about what you've been taught." Something like that.

Instead, the translator gets one unit of translated expression for each unit of text—and may indicate a few alternative readings only in footnotes. The translator's responsibility militates against ambivalence.

The paradigm of translation shapes the behavior of biblical interpreters, however, even when they're off translation duty. Our articles and essays promulgate the assumption that we're restricted, in our interpretive reading, to a single best option for apprehending any given passage from the Bible. Our exegetical arguments assert with vigor that now, at last, we've detected the decisive clue for clarifying interpretations that have eluded two thousand years of close readers. We treat the biblical texts as cryptograms with a concealed key that, once discovered, will reveal a recognizably definite correct answer beyond any shadow of disagreement. Yet disagreements remain, demonstrating by their very durability that the mirage of textual determination has again retreated beyond the grasp of its pursuers, however brilliant, however faithful.

Even the goal of "fidelity" to the biblical text, sometimes used as a guide in cases of radical cultural and linguistic difference, can sometimes be haunted by the perfect-translation fantasy. A rich notion of "fidelity" embraces far more than grammar and lexicography, but when a particular paraphrase or a new-media representation of a biblical passage dissatisfies its biblical scholars, they are apt to attribute their frustration to the "free-ness" of the paraphrase, or the remoteness of the video production from the biblical text: "That's not what the biblical text *really means.*" We should, however, distinguish the matter of "free paraphrase" or of the metaphorical distance that separates two media from the matter of "fidelity"; as translators have long known, one may sometimes attain the greatest fidelity to a biblical expression only by a very free paraphrase, and one might argue that the stunning intensity of passages from Ezekiel or Revelation are more effectively communicated with images than with words.

Words in the Way

One unfortunate result of the dominant model of interpretation as translation lies in the persistent mystification of verbal communication, which practitioners of biblical studies often limit to print communication (as though there were no noteworthy distinction between oral words, handwritten words, and printed words). Scholars collaborate in perpetuating a myth that (printed) words are a unique, semi-divine product with unearthly qualities. Because (printed) words do such an admirable job of facilitating communication, scholars have often jumped to the conclusion that words must possess special properties that constitute them as a uniquely appropriate medium for expression, imbued with "meaning" in something of the way that scientists once believed that combustible materials were imbued with a fiery essence, or that sleep aids contained sleepiness. If words work, these scholars reason, they must work on the basis of intrinsic meanings.

The mystique of words derives further currency from theological reasoning. The first verse of John's gospel, the opening verses of Genesis, the genre of prophetic oracles, and the principal modes of Jesus' teaching (particularly his teaching in parables) seem to mark verbal communication as God's communicative medium of choice. The proposition that God's choice to make known the record of divine truth in verbal form, as writing, *Scripture*, then seems to warrant our regarding words as miniature vessels of potential revelation (whereas inductions from non-verbal visual phenomena, from sublime sound or heady scent, can be dismissed as forms of "natural theology").

To the contrary, however, words—spoken or written or printed—are not the unique vessels of meaning that our interpretive practices often imply them to be (even when we do not adhere to that premise self-consciously or explicitly). Not only words, but also physical gestures, non-verbal sounds, images, even smells convey meaning in ways different from, but associated with, linguistic expression. Our hermeneutics, preoccupied with the fantasy of the perfect translation, concentrate almost to the point of exclusivity upon words. Indeed, we concentrate not simply on words, but devote most of our attention to *printed* words.

Be it conceded right away that language has proven an inestimably versatile and effective means of communication. When my children have fallen asleep, I can often manage to make my ideas evident to my wife in gesticulation and grimace without spoken words, but I do not propose that words are a bad idea and should be abandoned, or that they are so radically ambiguous as to be indistinguishable from cubist paintings or thrash rock'n'roll. Words have made possible tremendous, powerful, convincing, highly-effective acts of communication. Indeed, we who are profoundly (decisively?) shaped by the effects of language can hardly imagine the scope and force of words' influence on every aspect of human life. Neither I nor anyone I know wishes to undervalue linguistic communication.

At the same time, I do not wish to *over*value language, ascribing to it mystical properties that go beyond the social conventions that give it currency. Communication does not depend on spoken or written language ("written" in the sense of spelled-out words). One can effect understanding on the basis of gestures, pictures, inarticulate sounds. If one allows a background dependence on language (as language itself generally depends on some sensuous acquaintance with the phenomenal world)—then communication can get on quite well without explicit recourse to verbal language, as speakers of sign language can testify. Drivers cannot usually speak directly to one another, but they find ways of communicating with car horns, gestures, and startling automotive maneuvers, and internationally recognized symbols guide drivers' navigation in areas where they do not understand the local language. Words form an extraordinarily strong, labile, productive medium for the social interactions that sustain meaningful connections among (other) words, images, sounds, experiences—but we need not posit the *necessity* of verbal language for such social connections. Some social conventions can sustain associations of meaning and experience even in the absence of verbal language.

That is to say, the success with which humans often use words to communicate does not imply that words constitute the quintessence of communication. Words prove especially useful for communicating particular kinds of information under particular circumstances, but their outstanding usefulness does not make an argument for their *necessity*. Neither ought we conclude that words provide a paradigmatic *mode* of communication, so that our theories of interpretation need only account for words in order to claim completeness. Once we entertain seriously the possibility that legitimate interpretation involves a great deal more than providing word-for-word alternatives, the power and the prominence of non-verbal communication oblige us to offer theories of interpretation that do not treat non-verbal interpretation as an incomplete, insufficient, primitive, non-scholarly offshoot of the (verbal) *real thing*. A hermeneutic that works only for words is *itself* incomplete and insufficient.

Nor does the theological argument for treating words as the paradigmatic instance of communication carry decisive weight. Though the Word became flesh and dwelt among us, the Word was not manifest as a part of speech or a dictionary entry; the Word effected communion with humanity by *becoming human*, not by becoming an inscription. The Bible foregrounds instances of verbal communication from God, but reports a variety of other means by which God makes the divine will known. God communicates not exclusively through (presumably) verbal communication, but also through visions and through physical demonstrations, and one would be foolhardy who determined that God might not communicate in yet other ways. The prophets received revelatory visions as well as verbal bulletins, and God commanded that they pass along their divine messages by physically enacted communication. Paul insists that the created order itself communicates something of God's identity in Romans 1. Indeed, those who construe the word *logos* in John's Prologue flatly as "word" oversimplify the semantic breadth of the term in Greek (as its common Hebrew partner, *dabar*, likewise covers much more semantic terrain than just "word"). This caveat applies all the more since John deploys the term in a setting that lacks the contextual markers that might tend sharply to limit plausible construals of that noun. The doctrine of the incarnation itself should serve as a warning that exclusively verbal revelation was not sufficient in itself; God chose *body English*, as it were, as the medium for the fullness of communication. Where Protestant theologies—which in some instances show a marked aversion to physical or sensuous dimensions of human life, preferring abstractions, thoughts, and words to images, matter, and action—prospered with the advent of printed communication and widespread literacy, other traditions have maintained the theological importance of communication in visual arts, in physical movement, in sound and smell and taste. While arguments for emphasizing verbal communication identify a legitimate strand of biblical and theological reflection, words should not be permitted to eclipse iconic, active, aural, olfactory, gustatory, and tactile aspects of theological discourse.

If we dispense with the mystical-vessel model of verbal meaning, we are not bereft of resources for explaining the relative stability of literary understanding, nor the effectiveness of verbal communication. Proponents of "meaning" often construct the hermeneutical alternatives only as: either "words *have meanings*" or "any word can mean any thing." This illegitimately excludes a pivotal range of middle terms that provide quite adequate accounts of communication. Words, as they are ordinarily used by ordinary communicators, typically elicit a very few predictable responses from ordinary audiences. One might think of several referents for the word "cup," depending on whether one participates actively in cooking, or waiting on tables, or on men's athletics, but few if any audiences will associate the word "cup" with a rabid wolverine (until now). The social conventions that undergird communication are strong, deep, and quite elastic (though not infinitely so). In most regards words are indeed more stable and effective a means of communication than other media. Other means of communication, however, have benefits of their own, as traffic signs, musical compositions, and fine cooking (or to remain in the sphere of theological practice, church architecture, hymnody, incense, the elements of communion, and even pot-luck suppers) all demonstrate.

Scholars have become accustomed to fixating so unwaveringly on words that they will espouse theories whose shakiness could readily be brought to light by framing them graphically. To choose a simple, common example, New Testament scholars frequently draw exegetical conclusions about the relative dates of documents or sayings by assaying the christologies that the texts reflect, or the degree to which the texts show concern about the delay of the parousia. They posit that when a text says, "Jesus is surely returning soon," it must be early (since it shows no doubt about the second coming), but when a text says, "He will surely come at some point, now or later," it must come from a later period (since it seems to allow for uncertainty concerning when Jesus will arrive). Such reasoning might be represented graphically by the charts in the accompanying figure. In each case, as a document's Christology moves toward a more exalted understanding of Christ, or as it shows a greater degree of anxiety over the return of the Lord, that document may be presumed to date from a later period.

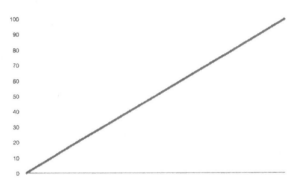

High Confidence   High Anxiety
of Jesus' Imminent Return   over Jesus' Imminent Return

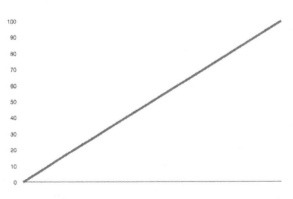

Low Christology   High Christology
(Jesus as human)   (Jesus as divine)

Of course, scholars sometimes need to fudge their relation to these (presupposed) charts, in order to bolster their own theories about dating documents. When a document that scholars are very sure about assigning to the late first century shows robust confidence that the Lord will come soon, said scholars can point out that the apparent confidence is intended to *allay the fears* of the community to which the text is addressed. When a supposedly late document includes a passage that evinces a low Christology, the passage in question may be *an older tradition* that the editors included intact. Conversely, when an early text shows signs of a high Christology, we may conclude that a later editor has emended the document.

Few scholars would uphold so bald a presentation of their reasoning. The practice of evaluating christological tone for dating New Testament texts presumably complements other, more rigorous criteria. Yet anyone who looks at these graphs and thinks hard about the geographical, theological, and cultural diversity that characterize the earliest years of the Christian movement must recognize how tenuous such criteria must be; *any* assumptions about a predictable correlation between chronology and either Christology or eschatology stand to falsify or mislead historical reason at least as much as they stand to aid it. A Galilean from whom Jesus of Nazareth exorcised a persistent demonic presence would probably hold to a higher Christology than a casual bystander who overheard snippets of a parabolic discourse, though both lived and reported their impressions of Jesus at the same time. A wandering Christian prophet might proclaim the nearness of the Day of the Lord just across town from a corner where a sage Christian teacher offered aphoristic counsel on how to live wisely and long.

The charts in the illustration are, of course, oversimplifications of more complex hypotheses. If one wanted to represent these hypotheses more fairly, one might, for instance, allow that anxiety over the delayed parousia was not a linear but a parabolic function. Or one might plot Christology against years in a scatter-chart, allowing for greater variability in the distribution of data. Then, however, one would run into the difficulty that scholars assign dates to the documents in question largely on the basis of the hypotheses that we are illustrating. The data points don't scatter much, because they have to a great extent been located with reference to the assumed validity of the hypothesis. While we can observe patterns of transition from one sort of outlook to another, the variety of particular circumstances and of human responses to those circumstances preclude our vesting the patterns we observe with the regularity that undergirds deductions about when or where or why. Sometimes visual representation of a hypothesis helps clarify just what the hypothesis entails, and how much credit that hypothesis deserves.

The question of visual representation, however, reaches beyond the value of interpreting historical-critical data and hypotheses with graphs or charts. Words are themselves sensuous phenomena, whether aural or visual. A word written is not simply the same as a word printed. A word printed in Bembo type is not simply the same as a word printed in Cooper Poster or Comic Sans. The way one presents a verbal message casts the message in a particular light; those who have read concert posters or other advertisements will have to acknowledge that not all words are presented equally—a point that fueled the transition from typewriting to computer word processing, from impact printers to laser and inkjet printers and high-resolution screens.

Hearing Meaning's Flavor

Words signify, in other *words*, not only by the letters that constitute the word, or by the meaning that we conventionally associate with the word, but also by the *appearance* of the word—and the visual context within which that word appears. René Magritte, the master teacher of the paradoxes of interpretation, wrought a career of painted and printed essays on just this aspect of the relation of words to images. He is best known for such works as "L'usage de la parole I" ("The Use of Words I"), a painting that combines the large painted image of a pipe with the written legend, "Ceci n'est pas un pipe" ("This is not a pipe"). The painting reminds viewers that the painting is not a pipe; it is a two-dimensional *representation*, significantly enlarged, of a three-dimensional implement. Further, the painting may prompt viewers to recognize that the words *un pipe* (and the demonstrative *Ceci*) are not a pipe, either. Verbal language and graphic illustrations offer two means for representing objects, concepts, and relations, but these media do not escape their status as representations.

Ceci n'est pas une Bible

In another work, Magritte notes, "In a painting, the words are of the same substance as the images." In yet another, Magritte reminds his reader that "An object never serves the same purpose as its name or its image."[2] Magritte's art of words and images challenges a reader's propensity to think of words as ontologically distinct from images, as possessing intrinsic properties associating themselves with their referents or rendering them particularly efficacious for interpretation. Had Magritte been particularly interested in biblical interpretation, he might seventy years ago have begun reminding his readers of the long-standing tradition of interpretation in statuary, in stained glass, in woodcuts, in icons; our sense of the breadth of biblical interpretation might already have extended to cope not only with Milton, Mozart, Doré, and Eichenberg, but also to

2. René Magritte, "Les mots et les images," *La Révolution surréaliste* 12 (December 15, 1929) 32–33.

Dali, DeMille, and Lloyd Webber (and in a more modest way, theologian/cartoonist Fred Sanders). The onrush of digital media's rich capacity for non-verbal communication, however, will make this point whether biblical scholars are prepared or not.

When we contemplate the kinds of differences that the future of electronic media will bear upon us, we can see all the more clearly the importance of learning how to relativize the importance of words in our disciplinary practice. Pictures, animations, and video will not *supplant* words, but they will become ever more prominent as supplement, as context. The interpretation of words alone will not suffice to account for this additional contextual matter. And interpretations *in* words alone will likewise seem increasingly paltry, when with so little extra effort one can illustrate one's remarks with three-dimensional virtual models of the synagogues of second-century Palestine, or dynamic diagrams of Solomon's social network, or animations of the dragon and the beast from Revelation. Our biblical interpretation will more closely resemble the kind Philip Dick described in *The Divine Invasion*:

> He spent some time with the holoscope, studying Elias's most precious possession: the Bible expressed as layers at different depths within the hologram, each layer according to age. The total structure of Scripture formed, then, a three-dimensional cosmos that could be viewed from any angle and its contents read. According to the tilt of the axis of observation, differing messages could be extracted. Thus Scripture yielded up an infinitude of knowledge that ceaselessly changed. It became a wondrous work of art, beautiful to the eye, and incredible in its pulsations of color.[3]

As academic biblical interpretation moves more rapidly and comprehensively into domains other than the printed word, practitioners will need to learn how to *evaluate* interpretations on unfamiliar terms. Under present circumstances, the dominant critical question posed to (verbal) interpretations consists principally in whether they appropriately honor the historical context of the text's origin; such questions well suit a discourse of interpretation that trades in verbal equivalency and verbal propositions as its currency. When interpretations involve not only verbal truth-claims about interpretive propositions, but also shapes, colors, soundtracks, and motion, the matter of historical verisimilitude recedes among a host

---

3. Dick, *The Divine Invasion* (New York: Pocket, 1981) 65–66.

of other questions. The questions that most obviously fit digital media interpretations are taken from the worlds of film criticism, art criticism, and literary criticism (though this latter appears in this context in a mode less concerned with authorial intent and "original audiences" than with contemporary assessments of literary effect).

How, for instance, will biblical scholarship cope with the question of depicting Jesus when the question applies not exclusively to high-budget commercial sand-and-sandal epics, but with a cornucopia of home-brewed instructional clips—or perhaps with a Jesus movie more comparable to Todd Haynes's *I'm Not There*, with six actors of varying races, ages, and genders portraying Jesus of Nazareth? Do we really want a Smell-o-vision representation of the stable in which Jesus may have been born? (Perhaps not until the magi arrive with their aromatic gifts.) Biblical interpreters will have to learn new critical sensibilities to match the new media with which we all deal.

Tasting Biblical Confections

These criteria feel awkward and subjective at present, but the effect of imprecision derives from inexperienced interpreters more than from the interpretive approaches. At an earlier moment when the cultural world of biblical interpretation also trembled and warped under the stress of impending technological revolution, anonymous scholars composed the woodblock compositions that became known as the *Pauper's Bible*. This late medieval mixture of graphic and verbal interpretations of the gospel combines images drawn from the Old Testament, from the Gospels, from pious legend and deuterocanonical narrative, to summarize a vast intertextual account of salvation history in forty woodcuts. The woodcuts themselves represent what Edward Tufte calls a "confection," a compilation of various sorts of images and information in a communicative ensemble whose whole vastly exceeds the sum of its parts.[4] Editions of the *Pauper's Bible* divide the printed (or hand-drawn) page into as many as eighteen small frames, each contributing a short text, the depiction of a character, or a scene from a biblical narrative (the number of frames in a given edition of the *Biblia Pauperum* may vary; one at hand shows twenty

---

4. Edward Tufte, *Visual Explanations: Images and Quantities, Evidence and Narrative* (Cheshire, CT: Graphics, 1997) XX.

frames, another twelve). The frames do not simply stack up figures and texts in a jumble; instead, the illustrations and quotations constitute an interpretive context for the gospel passage that the central panel depicts. The illustrations in one frame echo visual motifs from the others, calling attention to connections between the illustrated passages that are absent from the literal sense of the quoted passages. They show the biblical figures in clothing and situations proper to the fifteenth-century milieu of the woodcuts' composition, quietly making contemporary sense of the ancient writings. The careful arrangement of text and illustration—shaped by years of interpretive tradition and reproduction—express and encourage a harmonized interpretation of the Bible's message.

The *Pauper's Bible* intimates one direction for post–print-media confections of biblical interpretation today. Whereas modern biblical interpretation depends almost exclusively on the verbal medium of print, and its interpretive practices are haunted by the fantasy of a perfect translation, the Pauper's Bibles mingle form and color with text (handwritten text, in some versions, woodcut text, in others). When we compare this premodern multimedia interpretive exercise to its modern successors, we are likely to recognize that the *Pauper's Bible* lies closer to the frames, images, and text of a web page than do the lengthy expositions of contemporary academic scholarship. The woodcut images *show*, in rough strokes evoking easily imaginable scenes, a *sense* of the Bible, sensible to an audience more interested in the Bible than in scholars and their publications. Each individual frame connects to others via story line, back reference, future context, and so on. With a few digital-video clips, an audio backing track, and hyperlinks between the variously connecting pages, the fifteenth-century *Pauper's Bible* would fit the contemporary media environment more comfortably than does the twentieth-century *Journal of Biblical Literature*.

The anonymous evangelical confections of the *Pauper's Bible* bring us round, at last, to the second point I would press regarding the future of biblical interpretation as we modulate from a typographic interpretive culture to a digital-media interpretive culture. The *Pauper's Bible* testifies to the pivotal role that a disciplined imagination plays in biblical interpretation. For the past two centuries, interpreters' imaginations have been policed by criteria native to the discipline of historical analysis; other approaches have been permitted to extend the range of biblical interpretation, to add a second interpretive dimension, only so long as they orient themselves toward the pole-star of historical soundness. Thus, literary criticism of the Bible frequently highlights the supposed editorial seams that enable historical interpreters to isolate distinct strands of a tradition; social-scientific interpreters foreground the social conventions of the ancient Near Eastern and Hellenistic cultures from which the Testaments emerged. Historical reason determines the modern limits of legitimate interpretation. Imaginations informed by digital media will not sit still for the ponderous police work of historical authentication. New media will oblige interpreters to extend the range of their interpretive and critical faculties—and the further our endeavors extend from the exclusively verbal interpretive practice of contemporary biblical scholarship, the less pertinent the fantasy of perfect translation and the *imprimatur* of historical verification will seem. New media will teach us new criteria. But as the *Pauper's Bible* reminds us that the work of biblical interpretation has in past times communicated well in images, so the allegorical imagination that funded the *Pauper's Bible* can provide clues the directions that critical interpretation may take in new media.

Questions

1. Describe (or imagine) circumstances in which you communicated an important message without using words, or by inflecting your words with aural or visual accents. How did you expect your audience to recognize significance of the non-verbal part of the message?

2. Examine the picture of a book, included in this essay. Is it a Bible? In what ways would you say it "is" or "isn't"? What makes something "a Bible"?

3. Imagine a twenty-first-century "confection" (in the sense described in this essay) of biblical interpretation: a collage of texts, illustrations, interpreters, parallel texts, and commentary. Sketch (or execute) an example of such a page. How would such a page be useful to a reader? In what ways would such a page be deficient?

SELECTED BIBLIOGRAPHY

Alter, Robert. *The Art of Biblical Narrative*. New York: Basic, 1981.

Boomershine, Thomas E. *Story Journey: An Invitation to the Gospels as Storytelling*. Nashville: Abingdon, 1988.

Botha, Pieter J. J. "The Social Dynamics of the Early Transmission of the Jesus Tradition." *Neot* 27 (1993) 205–31.

———. "The Verbal Art of Pauline Letters: Rhetoric, Peformance and Presence." In *Rhetoric and the New Testament: Essays from the 1992 Heidelberg Conference*, edited by Stanley E. Porter and Thomas H. Olbrict, 409–28. Journal for the Study of the New Testament Supplements 90. Sheffield: Sheffield Academic, 1993.

Byroskog, Samuel. *Story as History, History as Story: The Gospel Tradition in the Context of Ancient Oral History*. Wissenschaftliche Untersuchungen zum Neuen Testament 123. Tübingen: Mohr/Siebeck, 2000.

Dewey, Joanna. "From Storytelling to Written Text: The Loss of Early Christian Women's Voices." *BTB* 26 (1996) 71–78.

———, editor. "Orality and Textuality in Early Christian Literature." *Semeia* 65 (1994).

———. "The Survival of Mark's Gospel: A Good Story?" *JBL* 123 (2004) 495–507.

Downing, F. Gerald. *Doing Things with Words in the First Christian Century*. Journal for the Study of the New Testament Supplements 200. Sheffield: Sheffield Academic, 2000.

Fivush, Robyn, and Catherine A. Haden, editors. *Autobiographical Memory and the Construction of A Narrative Self: Developmental and Cultural Perspectives*. Philadelphia: Erlbaum, 2003.

Fowler, Robert M. "The End of the Bible as We Know It: The Metamorphosis of the Biblical Traditions in the Electronic Age." In *Literary Encounters with the Reign of God: Festschrift for Robert C. Tannehill*, edited by Paul Kim and Sharon Ringe, 341–56. New York: T. & T. Clark, 2004.

———. "How the Secondary Orality of the Electronic Age Can Awaken Us to the Primary Orality of Antiquity, or What Hypertext Can Teach Us about the Bible." *Interpersonal Computing and Technology: An Electronic Journal for the 21st Century* 2.3 (1994) 12–46.

Hall, Mark. "The Living Word: An Auditory Interpretation of Scripture." *Listening* 21 (1986) 25–42.

Harvey, John D. *Listening to the Text: Oral Patterning in Paul's Letters*. Grand Rapids: Baker, 1998.

Hearon, Holly E. *The Mary Magdalene Tradition: Witness and Counter-Witness in Early Christian Communities*. Collegeville, MN: Liturgical, 2004.

Bibliography

Horsley, Richard A. *Hearing the Whole Story: The Politics of Plot in Mark's Story.* Louisville: Westminster John Knox, 2001.

Horsley, Richard A., Jonathan A. Draper, and John Miles Foley, editors. *Performing the Gospel: Orality, Memory, and Mark.* Minneapolis: Fortress, 2000.

Juel, Donald, "The Strange Silence of the Bible." *Interpretation* 51 (1997) 5–19.

Kelber, Werner. *The Oral and the Written Gospel.* 1983. Reprinted, Bloomington: Indiana University Press, 1997.

Krondorfer, Bjorn, editor. *Body and Bible: Interpreting and Experiencing Biblical Narratives.* Philadelphia: Trinity, 1992.

Labriola, Albert C., and John W. Smeltz, editors. *The Bible of the Poor [Biblia Pauperum].* Pittsburgh: Duquesne University Press, 1990.

Lee, Charlotte, and Frank Galati. *Oral Interpretation.* 7th ed. Boston: Houghton Mifflin, 1987.

Levy, Shimon. *The Bible as Theatre.* Sussex: Sussex Academic, 2002.

Loubser, Johannes A. "How Do You Report Something That Was Said With a Smile? Can we Overcome the Loss of Meaning when Oral-Manuscript Texts of the Bible are Represented in Modern Printed Media?" *Scriptura* 87 (2004) 296–314.

———. *Orality and Manuscript Culture in the Bible.* Stellenbosch, South Africa: Sun, 2007.

Malbon, Elizabeth Struthers. *Hearing Mark: A Listener's Guide.* Harrisburg, PA: Trinity, 2002.

Pelias. Ronald. *Performance Studies: The Interpretation of Aesthetic Texts.* New York: St. Martin's, 1992.

Rhoads, David. *Performance Criticism: An Emerging Discipline in New Testament Studies.* Eugene, OR: Cascade, 2009.

———, Joanna Dewey, and Donald Michie. *Mark as Story: An Introduction to the Narrative of a Gospel.* 2nd edition. Minneapolis: Fortress, 1999.

Roloff, Leland. *The Perception and Evocation of Literature.* Glenview, IL: Scott, Foresman, 1973.

Rubin, D. C., editor. *Remembering Our Past: Studies in Autobiographical Memory.* London: Cambridge University Press, 1996.

Schachter, Daniel L. *The Seven Sins of Memory: How the Mind Forgets and Remembers.* New York: Houghton Mifflin, 2001.

Shiner, Whitney. *Proclaiming the Gospel: First-Century Performance of Mark.* Harrisburg, PA: Trinity, 2003.

Soukup, Paul A., and Robert Hodgson, editors. *From One Medium to Another: Communicating the Bible through Multimedia.* Kansas City: Sheed & Ward, 1997.

Stein, R. H. "Is Our Reading the Bible the Same as the Original Audience's Hearing of It? A Case Study in the Gospel of Mark." *Journal for the Evangelical Theological Society* 46 (2003) 63–78.

Swanson, Richard W. *Provoking the Gospel: Methods to Embody Biblical Storytelling through Drama.* Cleveland: Pilgrim, 2004.

Tufte, Edward R. *Beautiful Evidence.* Cheshire, CT: Graphics Press, 2006.

Wansbrough, Henry, editor. *Jesus and the Oral Gospel Tradition.* JSNTSup 64. Sheffield: JSOT Press, 1991.

Wire, Antoinette. *Holy Lives, Holy Deaths: A Close Hearing of Early Jewish Storytellers.* Studies in Biblical Literature 1. Atlanta: Scholars, 2002.